Christopher Given-Wilson is Emeritus Professor of Medieval History at the University of St Andrews. His writing and research focuses on fourteenth- and fifteenth-century England.

CHRISTOPHER GIVEN-WILSON

Edward II

The Terrors of Kingship

PENGUIN BOOKS

PENGUIN BOOKS

UK | USA | Canada | Ireland | Australia
India | New Zealand | South Africa

Penguin Books is part of the Penguin Random House group of companies
whose addresses can be found at global.penguinrandomhouse.com.

First published by Allen Lane 2016
First published in Penguin Books 2019
001

Set in 9.5/13.5 pt Sabon LT Std
Typeset by Jouve (UK), Milton Keynes
Printed and bound in Great Britain by Clays Ltd, Elcograf S.p.A.

ISBN: 978-0-141-98991-4

www.greenpenguin.co.uk

Contents

For Rosalind, with love and gratitude

Preface

Son of a famous father, father of a famous son, Edward II (1307–27) presided over a twenty-year interlude of infamy bisecting a century during which the English monarchy established itself as the foremost military power in Western Europe. Edward I (1272–1307), conqueror of Wales and hammer of the Scots, came as close as any medieval king to uniting the British Isles under English rule. Edward III (1327–77) terrorized and humiliated both the French and the Scots, captured and imprisoned their kings and made English arms a byword for fame and glory abroad. It was by such standards that medieval kings were judged, but Edward II was a failure by any standards. The price he paid was to be the first English king since the Norman Conquest to be deposed.

That there was a tendency for strong and successful kings to be succeeded by weak and unsuccessful ones is one of the commonplaces of medieval English history: Edward I was followed by Edward II, Edward III by Richard II, Henry V by Henry VI, and so on. The anonymous author of the *Vita Edwardi Secundi* (Life of Edward II), in many respects the shrewdest of the early fourteenth-century chroniclers, contrived to see this as providential, enabling the brilliance of a great man to shine more brightly against a gloomy background.[1] Modern historians are more inclined to ask how sustainable it was for the resources of the medieval English state to be mobilized in support of effectively unlimited expansionist policies. Although the population of England, at around six million, comprised 75 per cent of the inhabitants of the British Isles, it was only about a third of that of France. Edward I, Edward III and Henry V may have built their reputations on conquest, but what they left to their successors were unfinished and arguably unwinnable wars and a kingdom groaning under the burden of taxation. Edward II's legacies from his father included debts of around £200,000, a burgeoning insurrection in Scotland and, after a decade of conflict, a precarious peace with France.

Yet, *damnosa hereditas* as this was, it was by no means untypical, for most kings faced not dissimilar problems. To overcome them they needed to cultivate the goodwill of the magnates, and in this respect the auguries at Edward II's accession in 1307 were favourable. The new king was twenty-three – no beardless youth, but still in the prime of life – his father's undisputed heir, and surrounded by a loyal and vigorous clutch of young earls. Always an exclusive group in the Middle Ages, the English earls numbered just ten in 1307, two of whom (Oxford and Richmond) were political lightweights. Of the remainder, Henry of Lincoln was fifty-six, but all the rest were between sixteen and thirty-five, broadly the same generation as the king. The greatest of them by birth and wealth were Edward's cousin, Thomas of Lancaster, and his nephew, Gilbert of Gloucester, and the remaining five – Humphrey of Hereford, Aymer of Pembroke, Guy of Warwick, Edmund of

Arundel and John of Warenne – were no parvenus, each of their earldoms having been in the family for at least one generation.

The personal and political relationships between them and the king formed the keystone of the political edifice. To raise armies, secure taxes, maintain law and order – in other words, to govern – he needed their active co-operation. Not only were they his natural advisers, deputies and comrades-in-arms, they were also the pre-eminent peers of Parliament, an institution still in its infancy, which might or might not include the embryonic 'Commons' but was at all times dominated by the Lords. Alongside the earls, sharing their dignity though not their private landed and military power, were the twenty-one bishops of England and Wales, several of whom combined high office in the royal administration with their pastoral duties, while below the earls in the lay hierarchy came the barons, a fluctuating group of up to two hundred men, only a small number of whom were politically active although most were militarily active. These were the men – the earls, bishops and barons – with whom a medieval king had to establish a modus operandi. It was his inability to do so that lay at the heart of Edward II's failure.

N

| 1 Northallerton |
| 2 Rievaulx Abbey |
| 3 Ripon |
| 4 Boroughbridge |
| 5 Myton-on-Swale |

Dundee
Perth
St Andrews
Stirling
Forth
Edinburgh
Dunbar
Glasgow
Berwick
Roxburgh
Bamburgh

Lochmaben
Dumfries
Corbridge
Tynemouth
Newcastle
Carlisle
Lanercost
Durham
Solway
Penrith
Darlington
Richmond
Scarborough
Copeland
1 •2
3 •
Furness
4••5
Lancaster
Lune Valley
Skipton
Ribble Valley
York
Preston
Wharfedale
Pontefract
Airedale

0   50 miles
0   100 km

Southern Scotland and Northern England
in the Reign of Edward II

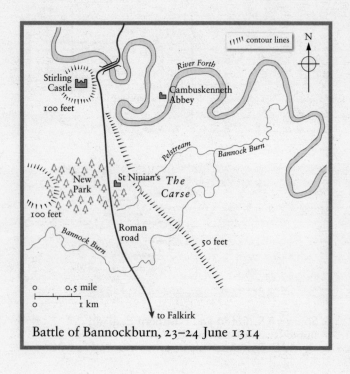

Battle of Bannockburn, 23–24 June 1314

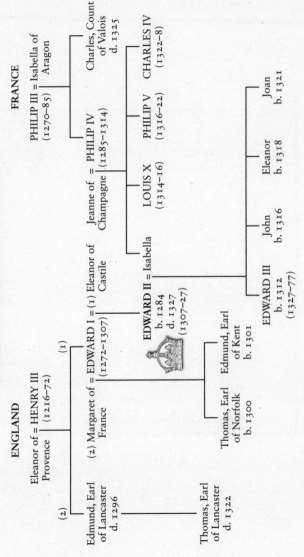

KINGS OF ENGLAND AND FRANCE

ENGLAND

Eleanor of = HENRY III
Provence   (1216–72)

(1)

Margaret of = EDWARD I = (1) Eleanor of Castile
France   (1272–1307)

EDWARD II = Isabella
b. 1284
d. 1327
(1307–27)

Thomas, Earl   Edmund, Earl
of Norfolk   of Kent
b. 1300   b. 1301

EDWARD III
b. 1312
(1327–77)

(2)

Edmund, Earl
of Lancaster
d. 1296

Thomas, Earl
of Lancaster
d. 1322

FRANCE

PHILIP III = Isabella of
(1270–85)   Aragon

Charles, Count
of Valois
d. 1325

Jeanne of = PHILIP IV
Champagne   (1285–1314)

LOUIS X   PHILIP V   CHARLES IV
(1314–16)   (1316–22)   (1322–8)

John   Eleanor   Joan
b. 1316   b. 1318   b. 1321

Edward II

I
'My Brother Piers'

This Edward [II] was a handsome man of great strength, but unconventional in his behaviour. For, shunning the company of the nobility, he preferred that of jesters, singers, actors, carters, diggers, oarsmen, sailors and other mechanics. He drank too much, betrayed confidences too easily, struck out without provocation at those standing around him and followed the counsel of others rather than his own. He was extravagant and splendid in his lifestyle, voluble, inconstant, unlucky against his opponents, and treated members of his household savagely. However, he was passionately attached to one person above all, whom he cherished, exalted, honoured and showered with gifts. The result of such infatuation was that both the lover and the loved were held in odium, the people scandalized and the kingdom brought to ruin.[1]

The testimony of Ranulf Higden (d. 1364), the most widely read chronicler in late medieval England, does not stand alone. Addiction to favourites, an alarming propensity for violence and a predilection for 'rustic pursuits' were characteristics often ascribed to Edward II. Seeking out the company of the low-born, he took positive pleasure in 'boorish occupations' – thatching roofs, driving carts and rowing boats. After Bannockburn, Scottish women taunted the English and their king by singing an oarsman's song, 'Heavalow, Rumbalow', while a royal messenger was reprimanded for saying that instead of winning battles or hearing Mass Edward preferred 'idling, making ditches and digging'.[2] The following year, the king nearly drowned while rowing in the Fens with 'a great company of simple people'; on another occasion he lost a belt swimming in the Thames. Carpenters and sailors were invited to dine in his chamber. Even Pope John XXII marvelled at the king's 'puerile frivolities'.[3] Whether Edward's interest in these quirky obsessions was competitive or simply companionable is unclear, but he seems to have laboured under an almost childlike misapprehension about the size of his world. Had greatness not been thrust upon him, he might have lived a life of great harmlessness.

The contrast with the traditional preferences of English rulers for the 'noble' pursuits of jousting, hunting and hawking could not have been starker, especially given that Edward was both physically imposing and a skilled horseman. It was his father, inevitably, to whom he was most frequently compared. Energetic and forceful in nature, Edward I could certainly be overbearing, but no one doubted his kingly qualities. His thirty-five-year reign had seen him crusade in the Holy Land, conquer Wales, come within touching distance of subjecting the Scots, enforce the rights of the crown to the hilt and reinvigorate the royal administration and legal system. Yet as his end approached he cannot have failed to be aware that his achievements were in jeopardy: wars and debts multiplied, and the old king's relations with both his nobles and his heir became increasingly strained. Edward I in his later years was an irascible and domineering figure, and what we know of their relationship suggests that his son found him frightening. Yet Edward II was easily frightened. One chronicler described him as 'always living in fear, afraid of his familiars and even of his friends, as if they were enemies'. He was haunted as much by the future as by the past.[4]

Edward II was born on 25 April 1284 at Caernarvon, where his father was putting the finishing touches to his conquest of Wales. As the fourteenth child of the king and his Spanish queen, Eleanor of Castile, he only became his father's heir as a result of the unusually cruel fortune (even by the standards of the age) that deprived his parents of more than half of their children, including all three of Edward's elder brothers, before they reached the age of twelve. Edward himself, however, grew up healthy, tall, muscular and athletic, renowned for his equestrianism – he 'managed his steed wonderfully well', said a contemporary poet – and reputed to be an excellent judge of horses. A letter he wrote in 1305 to his cousin Louis, Count of Evreux, hints at this as well as suggesting that he did not lack wit. 'We send you,' he joked, 'a big ambling palfrey which can hardly stand up, some of our bandy-legged harriers from Wales, who can easily catch a hare if they find it asleep, and some of our running dogs, who go at a gentle pace; for we are well aware that you delight in lazy dogs.'[5]

Later, as king, Edward sometimes displayed a propensity for sarcasm, and he always enjoyed the company of people who made him laugh. He also had a reputation for laziness, or at least a lack of application: he disliked getting out of bed in the morning, which on one occasion caused him to be late for an appointment with the King of France, and found the daily routine of government tedious. His habit of firing off verbal orders without written confirmation may be symptomatic of this, and sometimes led to administrative confusion.[6]

Despite being born into a large family, Edward was not brought up in a close familial environment. Shortly after his second birthday, his mother and father went to Gascony for three years, where the king was keen to re-establish control of England's continental province. A year after their return Queen Eleanor died, followed six months later by the young boy's grandmother, Eleanor of Provence, an unpopular figure but an affectionate family matriarch. During the 1290s three of his surviving sisters left England following marriages to continental nobles. The most influential figure in his boyhood was probably his master (*magister*) Guy Ferre, a Gascon knight who had spent many years in the service of both his mother and grandmother and who probably taught him to ride. Edward's preference throughout his life seems to have been for physical rather than cultural activities. If he developed any serious interest in art, literature or fashion, the evidence for it has not survived: as king, his court was 'neither distinctive nor innovatory'. However, he was an active patron of university education at both Oxford and Cambridge, from which came many of the clerks who served in the royal administration.[7]

By the time Edward was six – and now heir to the throne – thoughts were turning to the question of his marriage, the criterion for which would naturally be England's need for diplomatic alliances. In April 1290 he was betrothed to Margaret, the 'Maid of Norway', the seven-year-old heiress to the Scottish throne, but six months later, before they could even meet, she died, and with her the king's hopes of a dynastic union of the English and Scottish crowns. Baulked of this prize, Edward I turned his attention in the mid 1290s to the daughter of his ally the Count of Flanders, but this served only to enrage King Philip IV of France – with whom Edward was at war at the time – who bullied the count into sending the girl to Paris, where she was detained *sine die*. Eventually, in 1299, it was proposed that, to facilitate an Anglo-French peace, the young Edward should marry the French king's four-year-old daughter, Isabella, and in 1303 they were betrothed, although they did not marry until after he succeeded to the throne. With adolescence also came political responsibility. When Edward I went to Flanders in August 1297 to pursue his quarrel with Philip IV, he left his thirteen-year-old son as regent, but the king's arbitrary demands for men and money for his campaign provoked a violent backlash, and by October the young Edward and his advisers were obliged to barricade themselves behind the London city walls. A compromise was eventually reached with both Philip IV and the disaffected English nobles, but the incident should have been an early lesson in the limitations of royal power.

The Anglo-French détente of 1297 allowed Edward I during the last decade of his life to focus his energies on Scotland, where uncertainty about the succession following the Maid of Norway's death gave him the opportunity to convert long-voiced English claims to overlordship into something more tangible. Initially this involved little more than heavy-handed and unwelcome interference, but with time it became a war of conquest. In 1296, losing patience with what he saw as Scottish recalcitrance, Edward I deposed John Balliol, the king whose election he had supported four years earlier, removed the Stone of Scone to Westminster and suspended the Scottish monarchy. Thus began the Scottish Wars of Independence. Eight English armies, six of them led by the king in person, invaded Scotland in the course of the next decade in an increasingly brutal campaign to bring the Scots to heel. By 1305, it seemed as if this blitzkrieg had succeeded: William Wallace was caught and executed; the great majority of Scottish nobles and prelates submitted; the major strongholds of southern and eastern Scotland were in English hands; the administration of the 'land' (no longer a 'realm') was controlled from Westminster and a commission was set up to review Scottish law. This was, arguably, the moment at which the prospect of the 'English Isles' – an empire or even kingdom incorporating Wales, Scotland and Ireland as well as England – came closest to being realized during the medieval period: a moment for the ageing king to savour, if only a brief one.[8] The creation in 1301 of his sixteen-year-old son as Prince of Wales – the first heir to the English throne to bear that title – underlined the point.

It was in Scotland that the prince gained his first taste of warfare, campaigning for long periods between 1300 and 1306, sometimes with his father, but increasingly as commander of his own forces. Not that Edward I was a man to allow his son much latitude. If the young Edward occasionally presided over parliaments or acted as regent in his father's absence, he always knew (or should have known) that if he stepped out of line the leash would quickly be tightened – which was what happened. In June 1305, the prince uttered 'gross and harsh words' to Walter Langton, Bishop of Coventry and Lichfield and treasurer of the realm, after Langton accused him of breaking into one of his parks. Behind this doubtless lay deeper resentments, for the prince had just passed his twenty-first birthday and was probably chafing at his continued financial dependence on the crown, but the king reacted with fury. Langton had been his treasurer in difficult circumstances for ten years, and Edward I sprang to his defence, banishing his son from court, confiscating his seal and suspending payments to his 150-strong household. For the next few weeks, the prince was deprived of most of his servants and reduced to following behind his father 'at a distance of ten or twelve leagues' until the storm blew over. Not until mid October did he return to court.[9]

One of the penalties imposed on the young Edward during this quarrel was separation from his friends, which he described in a letter to his sister Elizabeth as 'anguish', asking her to intercede with their father to allow two of his servants in particular to rejoin him.[10] One of these was a Gascon esquire called Piers Gaveston. A year or two older than the prince, Piers was the second son of Arnaud de Gabaston, a baron of Béarn in southern Gascony who had served Edward I for twenty years before his death in 1302. It was in his father's company that Piers first came to England in 1296, initially serving in Flanders before joining the prince's household around 1300. By 1303, when he accompanied him to Scotland, he had become young Edward's companion (*socius*) rather than simply his esquire. Charming, vain, acquisitive and tactless, Gaveston soon gained an unshakeable hold on the prince's affections, and when the prince and some two hundred and fifty scions of the nobility were knighted in a spectacular dubbing ceremony at Westminster on 22 May 1306, Gaveston was among them. Before long, however, Piers's indiscretions came to the attention of the king. In 1306, after Robert Bruce murdered his rival John Comyn and declared himself King of Scots, thereby wrecking the previous year's settlement, Gaveston accompanied the prince northwards and helped him recapture Lochmaben Castle, but in October Piers withdrew from Scotland without the king's permission, together with twenty-one other young braves seeking to attend tournaments in France. Edward I was furious, branding them deserters and ordering the seizure of their lands.

What happened next demonstrated just how far matters had gone between Gaveston and the prince. Soon after Christmas, the king was persuaded by his new young wife, Margaret of France, to forgive the escapade, but although Gaveston was included along with the other twenty-one in the pardon issued on 13 January 1307, six weeks later he was banished from the kingdom. The catalyst for this was apparently an interview between the king and his son at which the prince asked that some great honour – perhaps Ponthieu (in northern France, but held by the English), perhaps the earldom of Cornwall – be bestowed on his favourite. 'You want to give lands away? You, who never won any?' expostulated Edward I, before seizing hold of his son and throwing him out of the room.[11] Yet the terms of Gaveston's exile were not harsh. He was to leave England by 30 April, return to Gascony and remain there until recalled; in the meantime, he was granted a generous £66 a year to support himself. The offence, it seems, was not his: the king simply wished to remove him from the presence of the prince, who could not be trusted to restrain himself.

Gaveston never did return to Gascony. Loaded with gifts, including five horses, two suits of armour for jousting, at least sixteen tapestries, hundreds of pounds in cash and much else, he was accompanied by the prince as far as Dover, whence he crossed with twenty servants to Ponthieu and spent the next three months jousting, entertaining and waiting. The prince, who remained in London, made plans to visit him, but this proved unnecessary. Edward I had stayed in the north during the winter of 1306–7, holding his last parliament at Carlisle in January. Unbending in his determination to subdue the Scots, despite barely being able to ride, he led his army out of the city on 3 July, but could travel no more than two miles a day. He died, in the arms of his servants, on 7 July 1307 at Burgh-by-Sands.

For the next five years, whatever wars were fought or left unfought, alliances made or unmade, administrative reforms drafted or constitutional principles advanced, there was no doubt in the minds of contemporaries that the great fault-line in English politics was the new king's relationship with Gaveston. It was hinted, though not unambiguously, that this was homosexual. Chroniclers described Edward's familiarity with Gaveston as 'excessive', 'inordinate', 'undue', 'improper', 'beyond measure and reason'. 'In love,' declared one, 'our king was incapable of moderation.' Robert of Reading, a deeply hostile chronicler writing at Westminster at the end of the reign, described the king's attachment to 'illicit and sinful unions' which led him to neglect the embraces of his wife, but in fact Edward did not entirely reject his wife, nor other women: Queen Isabella bore four children by him, and he fathered at least one bastard son.[12] Gaveston also fathered one legitimate and at least one illegitimate daughter.

Edward may have been bisexual, but it is also possible that he and Gaveston had concluded a formal compact of brotherhood-in-arms. The author of the *Vita* stated that the king 'had adopted [Gaveston] as his brother'; an anonymous chronicler declared that Edward 'felt so much love for him that he entered into a compact of brotherhood with him and decided to tie himself to him, against all mortals, in an unbreakable bond of affection'. Writs and letters from the king frequently described Gaveston as 'our dear brother'.[13] Such compacts were not uncommon at the time, usually in a military context, without any connotations of homosexuality, although the wisdom of a king-in-waiting becoming the brother-in-arms of a man whom many of the nobles regarded as a foreign upstart was questionable. It is of course quite possible that the two men were sworn brothers *and* lovers, but what was clear to all was that, for one reason or another, the king was infatuated. 'I never heard,' commented one chronicler, 'that one man so loved another.'[14] Edward listened only to Gaveston's advice, allowed him to control the flow of royal patronage, exalted him far beyond his deserts and could scarcely conduct the kingdom's business without him. Whether they were brothers, lovers or both, what mattered about their relationship was its political ramifications.

Barely had the new reign begun when the latter became all too clear. Within days if not hours of hearing of his father's death, Edward recalled Gaveston to England, and the first charter he issued, on 6 August 1307 at Dumfries, bestowed upon Piers the earldom of Cornwall, a title which Edward I had intended for one of the sons of his second marriage and which brought with it £4,000 a year of landed income. Three months later Gaveston married the king's niece, Margaret de Clare, sister of the Earl of Gloucester, and around this time Edward also made Gaveston his chamberlain, thus enabling him to control access to the king.[15] At a stroke, the 'Gascon upstart' was vaulted into the topmost rank of the English nobility and admitted to the inner circle of the royal family and household. His influence was unchallengeable: 'If any of the earls or magnates sought the king's special grace with regard to any business, the king sent him to Piers.' There were, in effect, 'two kings in one kingdom'.[16] To celebrate his new status – 'to enhance Piers' – a tournament was held in his honour at Wallingford on 2 December, where he compounded his sins by defeating the Earls of Arundel, Hereford and Warenne in the lists. A few days before Christmas, Edward announced that, when he crossed to Boulogne to marry Isabella, Gaveston would act as keeper of the realm in his absence. 'What an extraordinary thing,' observed the author of the *Vita*, 'that a man who was recently an exile and outcast from England has now been made governor and keeper of the same land.'[17]

Edward and Isabella were married at Boulogne on 25 January 1308 and returned to England two weeks later to prepare for their coronation, though by now the magnates' patience was running out. The ceremony was scheduled for 18 February, but a party led by the veteran Henry of Lincoln and backed by the brothers and youngest son of the French king, who had accompanied Isabella to England for the celebrations, demanded that before being crowned Edward must agree to banish Gaveston. Despite a week-long postponement to allow time for compromise, Edward would promise no more than that he would 'in good faith undertake whatever they said in the next parliament'.[18] The addition of an extra clause to the traditionally three-fold coronation oath, in which Edward swore to abide by 'the rightful laws and customs which the community of the realm shall have chosen', may have been designed to keep him to his word, although it might also have been drafted to try to limit the arbitrary measures introduced by Edward I during the previous decade.[19] Yet, whatever its intention, when the coronation took place on 25 February it was clear that Edward would not yield. Pride of place in the procession to Westminster Abbey went to Gaveston, who, dressed in royal purple 'like the god Mars', walked immediately before the king carrying the crown of St Edward. At the banquet that followed, Westminster Hall was hung with tapestries, not of the arms of England and France but of those of the king and his favourite, and Edward virtually ignored his new queen, instead spending the evening reclining on a couch with Gaveston.[20] What the twelve-year-old Isabella made of this is not recorded, but her uncles and brother were disgusted, venting their spleen to King Philip once they returned to Paris.

'And now, for the first time,' commented the author of the *Vita*, 'almost all the earls and barons of England rose against Piers Gaveston, binding themselves by a mutual oath never to rest until Piers had voided the land of England.'[21] Almost all, but not quite: two of the earls – Gaveston's brother-in-law, Gilbert of Gloucester, and, crucially, Thomas of Lancaster – still held back from the prospect of provoking civil war. Edward could also count on the support of the steadfast Hugh, the Elder Despenser, a baron of the first rank who had served his father with distinction for nearly two decades. Nevertheless, when Parliament met three days after the coronation it soon became clear that the demand for Gaveston's removal, led by 'Piers's greatest enemy and persecutor', the Earl of Lincoln, was undiminished.[22] When Edward prevaricated, the assembly broke up and both sides prepared for war, summoning their retainers, fortifying and garrisoning their castles. The king and Gaveston retired to Windsor, breaking behind them the bridges over the Thames at Staines and

Kingston, while their opponents gathered at Lincoln's castle of Pontefract to draft a remonstrance, the Three Articles. The distinction this made between the crown and the person of the king – the 'doctrine of capacities', here enunciated with unprecedented clarity – was employed to justify constraint of a ruler who 'is not guided by reason' and who was not therefore maintaining 'the dignity of the crown'. Gaveston, they declared – although he was not named but merely referred to as 'the person who is talked about' – was a sower of discord in the kingdom, a robber of the people and a traitor to the realm; he had already been attainted and judged, yet the king continued to maintain him 'against all men'. Since, however, Edward had sworn at his coronation 'to keep the laws that the people shall choose', he was bound to accept their judgment on this point – that is, to exile Gaveston.[23]

On 28 April, when Parliament reconvened, the Three Articles were presented to the king. Initially he continued to resist, but on 18 May, after Philip IV had written from Paris to add a father-in-law's voice to the demands for the favourite's expulsion, Edward gave way. Gaveston was to be banished from England in perpetuity and relinquish his earldom of Cornwall, and the Archbishop of Canterbury, Robert Winchelsey, pronounced sentence of excommunication on him should he return. In desperation, Edward decided at the last minute to make Gaveston Lieutenant of Ireland, and accompanied him to Bristol where, on 25 June 1308, he took ship for Dublin.

It would be a year before king and favourite were re-united. Gaveston seems to have been an effective military leader in Ireland – his soldierly abilities were never in doubt – but the paucity of contemporary comment on his activities there was symptomatic of the fact that the real challenges facing the king and the kingdom lay elsewhere. Barely had Gaveston departed when Edward announced his intention to lead a campaign to Scotland. In the event, this was soon abandoned, but the king had at least shown evidence of intent, and this, combined with a generally more conciliatory stance, succeeded in winning over some of the earls who had opposed him, Lincoln included. Yet, if Lincoln was biddable, there were ominous signs during the winter of 1308–9 of a rift between Edward and Lancaster, who may have got wind of the king's moves to secure Gaveston's return.

These had begun even before the favourite crossed to Ireland, with supplicatory letters to mollify Philip IV and beg Pope Clement V to absolve Gaveston from his sentence of excommunication should he return. By April 1309 Edward felt strong enough to propose to Parliament that his banishment be rescinded; this was rejected, and instead the king was presented with a petition for reform drafted by Lancaster, Hereford, Warwick and other earls and barons at a tournament at Dunstable a few weeks earlier. This focused on the legal and financial oppressions committed by royal ministers, especially the imposition of additional export duties and the abuse of the system of *prise*, or purveyance, which allowed provisions to be requisitioned for the king's household but was persistently extended to cover armies too, often with little prospect of repayment. There was nothing new about such grievances – much the same issues had been

at the heart of the crisis leading to the Confirmation of
the Charters in 1297 – but before a satisfactory compromise could be agreed, the Gaveston question once again
intervened. At the beginning of June 1309 the papal bull
absolving him finally arrived in England, and on 27 June
Piers crossed from Dublin to Chester, whither Edward
hurried to welcome him.

Initially it seemed as if the king had learned some lessons. At a parliament at Stamford in late July, Edward
agreed to limitations on his right of *prise* and a number of
other reforms, in return for which Gaveston was restored
to the earldom of Cornwall. Lancaster, however, who by
now was emerging as the leader of the opposition, absented
himself from Stamford, while Gaveston soon rediscovered
his knack for giving offence. It was around this time, so it
was said, that he coined nicknames for several of the earls:
Warwick, 'the black dog of Arden'; Lincoln, 'burst belly';
Pembroke, 'Joseph the Jew'; Lancaster, simply 'the churl'.[24]
The Scottish campaign was abandoned, and by October
several of the earls were refusing to attend a parliament at
Oxford because Gaveston would be present.

Another assembly was scheduled for February 1310, at
Westminster, but after an uneasy truce over the festive
period, which Edward spent with Gaveston at his favourite
manor of King's Langley (Hertfordshire), it became clear
that little had changed. When February came, Lancaster,
Hereford, Warwick and Pembroke obeyed the royal summons but remained in the city of London, refusing to come
to Westminster while Piers was 'skulking in the king's
chamber'.[25] The stand-off lasted three weeks, delaying the

start of Parliament until 27 February. When it did open, Edward was immediately presented with a petition for the establishment, for a limited period of eighteen months, of a commission with power to reform all aspects of royal government. Threatened with deposition if he refused to comply – and this, remarkably, less than three years on from his accession – he agreed on 16 March to the appointment of twenty-one Lords Ordainers: seven bishops, eight earls and six barons. They included friends as well as enemies of the king – though not, of course, Gaveston – but there was no doubting the humiliation for Edward in being forced in effect to surrender his power for a year and a half.

The ostensible reason for summoning Parliament had been to devise a strategy for dealing with Robert Bruce, and with domestic politics on hold while the Ordainers prepared the reform agenda, Edward now seized the moment. Taking Gaveston with him, not least to keep him out of harm's way, he went north in July and spent the autumn in Scotland, leading a 5,000-strong army through the borders to Glasgow, Renfrew, Linlithgow and Edinburgh, reinforcing garrisons and allegiances. Bruce was wise enough not to risk an engagement, and in November the king withdrew to Berwick, where he remained until July 1311. Hoping to prove his military worth to the sceptical English earls, Gaveston went back across the border in January 1311, but although he led an English force as far as Perth and Dundee, the Scots avoided him and the campaign fizzled out. Edward too was keen to lead another army into Scotland, but he lacked the resources to raise one and dared not risk summoning a parliament, while plans to bring troops across from Ireland never got off the ground. Little had been achieved, and rumours multiplied: the real reason for the campaign, said some at Westminster, was to sound out the possibility of Bruce offering Gaveston a refuge in Scotland should the need arise. The English king was certainly in contact with Bruce, and when he returned to London in July he left Gaveston as his lieutenant in Scotland, his base of operations the massive coastal stronghold of Bamburgh (Northumberland), well out of reach of his English enemies but within a day's ride of the border. Yet, when Bruce crossed the Solway in August to launch a raid into Tynedale, Gaveston lacked the resources to stop him, and a month later the Scottish king repeated the exercise, this time harrying Redesdale and burning Corbridge.

One of the reasons for the failure of the 1310–11 Scottish campaign was that the only earls apart from Gaveston who took part were Gloucester and Warenne, several of the others claiming that their responsibilities as Ordainers obliged them to remain in London. Lancaster in particular was by now irreconcilable: when his father-in-law, Lincoln, died in February 1311, he inherited the earldoms of Lincoln and Salisbury to add to the three he already held – Lancaster, Leicester and Derby – but to secure them he needed to pay homage and fealty to the king, traditionally performed in person. He duly travelled north in the spring, but refused to cross into Scotland, while Edward, a few miles away over the border, similarly declined to return to England. In the end the king gave way and crossed the Tweed, though only after an exchange of insults which almost erupted into violence, and although Lancaster performed his fealty, he refused even to speak to Gaveston. Ominously for the latter, the vast estates Earl Thomas now inherited more than doubled his annual income and inflated both his influence and his *hauteur* proportionately.

Meanwhile the Ordinances were being framed, chiefly by Lancaster, Hereford, Warwick, Pembroke and Archbishop Winchelsey. That they were in part motivated by hatred of Gaveston is beyond doubt, but there was much more to them than that. Containing forty-one clauses, they dealt with the whole range of governmental activity: the royal prerogative; the king's household; the collection and control of revenue; protection of the Church; the operation of the law courts; the appointment of central and local officials; parliamentary procedure and much else. Strict limits were placed on the king's freedom of action: he was forbidden to go to war, leave the realm, appoint ministers or make grants without the consent of the nobles in Parliament, and all his 'evil counsellors' were to be dismissed.[26]

Chief among the latter, inescapably, was Gaveston, not just an evil counsellor but a despoiler of the kingdom, an enemy of the people and a maintainer of malefactors who had arrogated royal power to himself and 'estranged the heart of the king from his lieges'.[27] The battle of wills over the favourite was joined once more. On his return from Scotland in August 1311, Edward was shown a copy of the Ordinances, which he promptly rejected. Weeks of wrangling eventually led him to make an offer: he would accept 'forever' everything that the Ordainers proposed if they would just 'stop persecuting my brother Piers and allow him to have the earldom of Cornwall'.[28] This in turn was rejected

by the earls, and once again the king was ground into sub-
mission. Published in St Paul's churchyard on 27 September,
the unexpurgated Ordinances became law in the following
month. Gaveston was to leave the realm by 1 November,
banished not only from England but also from all the king's
dominions 'forever, without returning'. If he disobeyed, he
would be 'treated as an enemy of the king and his people'.[29]

Yet disobey Gaveston did, spending barely two months
in the Low Countries before returning. It might have been
the birth of a daughter to his wife Margaret at York in
early January 1312 that induced him to come back, but
once in England it soon became clear that he had no intention of leaving. Nor did Edward encourage him to do so:
on 16 January he revoked the Ordinances, and two days
later restored Piers to his earldom. Neither man dared
come south, however, and the king was unwilling to allow
Piers to stray far from his presence. Once again civil war
loomed and giddy rumours abounded: the king, it was
said, would recognize Bruce as King of Scots or hand
Gascony to Philip IV in return for protecting Piers. By mid
March, Gaveston had been installed in Scarborough Castle,
which was garrisoned and provisioned for a siege and
offered escape by sea if necessary.

Meanwhile their enemies were gathering in London, where
on 13 March Archbishop Winchelsey declared Gaveston
excommunicated for having violated the Ordinances. Even
Gloucester and Warenne, moderates thus far, now committed themselves to securing his removal, and after taking an
oath of mutual support the earls and barons set out to track
him down. Two barons of the northern March (the Scottish

borderland), Henry de Percy and Robert de Clifford, were sent to the far north, while Gloucester patrolled the south, Hereford the east, Lancaster the west, and Pembroke and Warenne were sent to Yorkshire to apprehend the miscreant. Lancaster wrote to Edward demanding that Gaveston either be handed over to them or sent back into exile. Seeking a refuge, king and favourite decamped to Newcastle, but when Lancaster, Percy and Clifford arrived there on 4 May, they fled by ship back to Scarborough, abandoning arms, war-horses and a hoard of royal jewels in their haste.

Edward now made the mistake of leaving Gaveston while he went to York to raise troops, allowing Lancaster to interpose his force between them while Pembroke, Warenne, Percy and Clifford invested Scarborough. The siege lasted ten days, until on 19 May Gaveston agreed terms with them – or at least with Pembroke. Earl Aymer guaranteed Gaveston's safety until 1 August, during which time he would be taken to York where, in the presence of the king and Lancaster, discussions would be held; if no agreement was reached, he would be brought back to Scarborough. Sieges were often suspended in such fashion, but the terms were unduly favourable to an excommunicated 'enemy of the people', and some believed Pembroke to have been bribed by the king. Lancaster at any rate did not regard himself as bound by them.

A meeting was held at York from 26 to 28 May, but the only decision made was that a parliament would convene in July; in the meantime Gaveston remained in the custody of Pembroke. The latter vehemently denied responsibility for what happened next, but although he was probably not in collusion with Warwick and Lancaster, he was certainly guilty of negligence. Taking Gaveston south, ostensibly to keep him safe, he arrived on 9 June at Deddington (Oxfordshire), where, deciding to pay a visit to his wife at nearby Bampton, he left his charge in the rector's house with only a few guards. One way or another, news of Gaveston's whereabouts reached Warwick, who instantly gathered a force, rode through the night, and early on the morning of Saturday 10 June surrounded the rectory and awoke Gaveston with the cry: 'Arise, traitor, thou art taken!' Stripped of his belt of knighthood and followed by a jeering, trumpet-blaring mob, he was taken to Warwick Castle and thrown into jail. 'He whom Piers called Warwick the Dog has now bound Piers with chains,' declared the author of the *Vita*, and the black dog was running with a pack. Within a day or two Lancaster, Hereford, Arundel and several barons had arrived at Warwick to decide Gaveston's fate. The mortified Pembroke strove to recover his charge, but was told by Gloucester that he should have been more careful about what he agreed to. By 18 June, a decision had been reached. There was some sort of trial, or at least a tribunal, and oaths of mutual solidarity were sworn by those present, but it was primarily Lancaster who 'took upon himself the peril of the business'.[30] On the morning of 19 June, Gaveston was led out of Warwick Castle and along the road to Kenilworth as far as Blacklow Hill, which was on Earl Thomas's land. Without further ado, he was handed over to two of Lancaster's Welsh retainers, one of whom ran a sword through him and the other cut off his head.

2
King Hobbe and Cousin Thomas

The Gaveston years, 1307 to 1312, set the course of English politics for a decade. Soul-baring and humiliating for the king, they stripped him of his regal mystique and spread a poison through the arteries of the body politic that proved ineradicable as long as Edward occupied the throne; they brutalized and militarized political society; they gave rise to a reform programme that became the touchstone for baronial opposition; and they fatally undermined the English position in Scotland.

In the short term, moreover, Gaveston dead proved as divisive as Gaveston alive. Edward viewed his death as murder and was bent on revenge; to his killers, it was the judicial execution of an enemy of the people, justified by the Ordinances and by his excommunication. Yet it also split the opposition to the king: after June 1312, Pembroke and Gloucester immediately returned to the royalist camp, while Lancaster, Warwick and Hereford summoned their retainers and refused to attend Parliament. The stand-off lasted more than a year. Edward insisted that the jewels seized at Newcastle be returned, that there be no reference in any settlement to Gaveston as a traitor or miscreant, and that no action be taken against his followers. An agreement along these lines was brokered by Pembroke and other moderates in December 1312, and in February 1313 the Newcastle hoard was returned to the king, but the accord collapsed within weeks.

Realizing the weakness of his position, Edward now sought external help: he invited papal mediators to England, farmed the revenues of Gascony to Pope Clement V in return for a loan, and in late May 1313 crossed to Paris, where he and Isabella spent two months at her father's court. With Gaveston out of the way, the ageing Philip IV looked more benignly on his son-in-law, who by this time had fathered an heir, the future Edward III, born at Windsor in November 1312 – the only 'praiseworthy or memorable thing' the king had done in six years, said the author of the *Vita*.[1] The death of the curmudgeonly Archbishop Winchelsey in May 1313 also strengthened Edward's hand, allowing him to secure the appointment of his servant Walter Reynolds to the see of Canterbury. With the pope, the French king and the leader of the English Church behind him, Edward now felt strong enough to impose a settlement on the recalcitrant nobles. On 14 October 1313, after lengthy negotiations, those principally responsible for Gaveston's death (Lancaster, Warwick, Hereford, Arundel, Percy and Clifford) knelt before the king in Westminster Hall to receive his pardon, promising in return not to pursue Gaveston's adherents.[2] Neither Piers nor his followers were labelled as traitors, and no mention was made of the Ordinances. This did not give the king everything he wanted, but he had at least reasserted a measure of authority. With a grant of taxation and loans totalling £76,000 from Philip IV, the pope and the English Church, there now existed both the means and the opportunity to tackle the Scottish question.

This was not before time. The eighteen months following his uprising in February 1306, while Edward I still lived, had seen Bruce driven off the Scottish mainland to seek refuge in the Western Isles, three of his brothers executed, his sister, wife and daughter imprisoned, and English rule reimposed. However, Edward II's failure to maintain the momentum following his father's death had allowed 'King Hobbe [Fool]', as the English derided Bruce, to win support and credibility for his claims by starting to expel the English cuckoos from their Scottish nests. At the height of Edward I's power, the English and their supporters had held some forty castles in Scotland, from Caerlaverock and Roxburgh in the borders to Inverness and Elgin on the Moray Firth. By 1310, a quarter of these had fallen to Bruce, who was by now confident enough to start summoning his own parliaments – the first being held at St Andrews in March 1309. Edward II's 1310–11 campaign stemmed the tide temporarily, but by 1313 the Scottish recovery was in full spate once more. Between January 1313 and March 1314, Perth, Dumfries, Linlithgow, Caerlaverock, Edinburgh and Roxburgh all fell to Bruce's men. Their fortifications were razed to prevent them being reoccupied, and in November 1313 King Robert proclaimed that any Scottish landholder who refused to acknowledge his kingship within the next twelve months would suffer perpetual disinheritance.

Facing the total collapse of English support in Scotland, Edward II summoned an army to muster at Berwick by June 1314. Although the Earls of Lancaster, Warwick, Arundel and Warenne declined to serve in person – citing the fact that, contrary to the Ordinances, the king had not sought Parliament's permission to make war – Hereford, Gloucester and Pembroke responded to the summons, and Edward prepared the ground carefully, ordering plentiful supplies of provisions for what would turn out to be one of the largest English armies of the Middle Ages.

In March 1314, the English campaign was given added urgency when the captain of Stirling Castle, besieged by Bruce and his brother Edward, agreed that if no relieving army appeared by Midsummer Day, 24 June, he would surrender it. Even so, Edward II cut it fine. Not until the afternoon of 23 June did Bruce's men, straddling the old Roman road from Stirling to Falkirk, catch sight of the English army. Falling back towards the castle, the Scots took up a position on the fringe of an elevated area of woodland called New Park or St Ninian's Park (after the church located there), through which the road passed. A group of English knights, apparently expecting them to flee, rode forward on their great destriers to cut off the retreat, but found themselves facing greater odds than they had anticipated. Seeing Robert Bruce mounted on 'a little palfrey', Sir Henry de Bohun, the nephew of the Earl of Hereford, sought immortality by charging directly at him, but when a blow from Bruce's axe split his head in two he was obliged to settle for mortality. The remaining English knights were driven off by the pugnacious Thomas Randolph, whom Bruce had created Earl of Moray in 1312 and who had led the siege of Edinburgh. This discouraging start for the English, marred by quarrels between their leaders which Edward seemed unable to contain, persuaded him to call a halt for the day, although the only readily available space to camp required the crossing of 'an evil, deep, wet marsh', the Carse of Balquiderock. Passing the brief hours of darkness in their armour, their horses bitted and restless, the soldiers can have enjoyed little sleep. One who certainly did not sleep was Alexander de Seton, a Scottish knight in English service who, under cover of night, slipped across to tell the Scots of English disagreements and demoralization, strengthening Bruce's resolve to stand and fight.[3]

Early on the morning of 24 June, the English moved to a position between the Carse and New Park, about a mile and a half south of Stirling Castle. Behind them straggled the 'foul, deep, marshy' Bannock Burn, beyond that the loops and bogs of the River Forth.[4] It was a dangerous and ill-chosen spot, especially for an army as large as Edward's, which, at around 15,000, was probably about twice the size of Bruce's, for the strip of firm and open ground between marsh, woodland and burn was too narrow to allow large troop concentrations to manoeuvre easily. Sure enough, before the English divisions could draw up in formation, the Scottish infantry emerged from the woods and began to advance down the slope towards them. Although the 2,000 English cavalrymen were much better equipped than the Scots, Bruce's decision to pack his infantry into schiltrons – dense formations, bristling 'like a thick-set hedge' with twelve-foot pikes – paid dividends.

It was a tactic, said Sir Thomas Gray in his *Scalacronica*, that the Scots had learned from the Flemish, who in 1302 had employed such phalanx-formations to blunt the French cavalry at Courtrai, and it was similarly successful at Bannockburn. After an inconclusive exchange of volleys from the archers on each side, the Earl of Gloucester led an English cavalry charge, but the schiltrons stood firm; isolated and surrounded, the knights were dragged from their horses and either killed – as was the twenty-three-year-old Gloucester – or captured. Once again the English archers were brought forward, and they managed to thin the ranks of Scottish pikemen, but the further the schiltrons advanced, the more tightly the English found themselves 'crushed together, so that they could not move', hemmed in between the marsh, the Scots, and their own rearguard, which barely saw action.[5] What began as a crush soon became a retreat, then a rout, and finally a desperate flight. Hundreds of English drowned trying to cross the Bannock Burn or the bogs around the Forth.

Edward II, seeing that the day was lost and that he was now in real danger of being captured, tried to gain entry to Stirling Castle but was warned that it would have to be handed over to Bruce. Instead, he fled with a handful of bodyguards to Dunbar, chased by the Scottish king's boon companion and fearsome war captain, Sir James Douglas, before escaping in an open boat to Berwick – the town from which, ten days earlier, he had marched out, banners aloft, at the head of 15,000 men. That his flight brought shame upon both king and kingdom was undeniable, though it was claimed that he had fought 'like a lion', swinging his mace to good effect when some Scottish knights tried to seize his horse's reins, before being escorted from the field against his will by the Earl of Pembroke and others.[6] Pembroke also escaped, but Hereford only got as far as Bothwell Castle before being captured; he was released a few months later in exchange for King Robert's wife, daughter and sister, just one of scores of English knights and lords whose cash or hostage value enriched many a Scotsman, to say nothing of the thousands of pounds' worth of armour, weaponry, horses and valuables seized from the abandoned English baggage train. The Scottish knight John de Moray alone was said to have ransomed twenty-three English knights and several esquires. Stirling was immediately handed over to Bruce and, with the sole exception of Berwick, the remaining English strongholds in Scotland soon capitulated. 'Oh! Day of vengeance and misfortune, day of ruin and dishonour, evil and accursed day, not to be reckoned in our calendar,' lamented the author of the *Vita*.[7]

Battles on such a scale were rare in the Anglo-Scottish warfare of the time: only Falkirk (1298), Halidon Hill (1333) and Neville's Cross (1346), all English victories, bore comparison with the events of 24 June 1314. Around two hundred English knights – about one in seven of the knights in England – were killed at Bannockburn, just two on the Scottish side, but the real impact of the battle was psychological. Bruce's merciful treatment of his English prisoners and of Scotsmen who had opposed him – so different from the fate that would have awaited him and his men had they lost – further enhanced his reputation, most obviously by comparison with his self-styled 'overlord', whose weak leadership, absence of tactical acumen and ignominious flight were deplored and derided in equal measure. So confident had Edward II been of victory that he had brought along with him the Carmelite friar Robert Baston, 'the most famous poet in all England', to compose verses in celebration of the expected triumph; instead, Baston found himself among the captured and was obliged to laureate Bruce's victory – the prelude to a rich commemorative tradition epitomized by Burns's 'Scots, wha hae wi' Wallace bled', the fictional eve-of-battle exhortation by Bruce to stand firm against 'proud Edward's power'.[8]

What Bannockburn did not do, however, was end the war for independence. Never a reluctant warrior, despite his reputation, Edward remained determined to crush the 'rebels and traitors' north of the border, but this new blow to his reputation, coming hard on the heels of the Gaveston debacle, destroyed his chances of uniting the English polity under his leadership. Bannockburn was a political as well as a military disaster for Edward, and for the next few years, while the king and Lancaster vied for supremacy south of the border, Bruce was again left to consolidate his power. He seized the opportunity with both hands, taking the war not just to northern England with devastating effect but also to Ireland. The *Herschip* (hardship) of the north had begun with the Tynedale and Redesdale raids of 1311. Further attacks on the border counties followed in 1312–13, but after Bannockburn the Scots began penetrating far deeper into England. In August 1314, a party led by Edward Bruce and Thomas Randolph ravaged as far as

Richmond in Yorkshire before crossing the Pennines and returning via Carlisle. Wherever they went, they carried off cattle and prisoners, burned or trampled crops and seized valuables – except in Durham where the bishop's men paid tribute. Armed lightly and moving swiftly on small, tough horses (*hobins*), the Scots were back north of the border within three weeks. One northern annalist called it the *rabies Scoticana* (Scottish frenzy).[9]

In September 1314, three months after Bannockburn, Edward II held a parliament at York to which came both those who had made good their escape from Scotland and those who had refused to serve there – chief among the latter being the Earls of Lancaster and Warwick. Whether or not their absence was talked about in private as a factor in the English defeat, it was not mentioned in public: it was not their honour but the king's that was tarnished, and his opponents lost no time in seizing their opportunity. Once again Edward had to swear to uphold the Ordinances of 1311, which he had more or less ignored for the past two years, and within the next few weeks the chancellor and treasurer of the realm, several of the leading officers of the royal household and thirty of the forty sheriffs were replaced. Not all the resulting changes were unpalatable to the king, but the purge was an unmistakable statement of intent. Pembroke, a conciliatory presence who had been the king's chief councillor since Gaveston's death, was also superseded, although he retained the king's confidence and continued to be entrusted with sensitive diplomatic missions. Symbolic of Pembroke's decline was the fact that, on the day Parliament ended, a long-running dispute between him and Lancaster over three manors in Northamptonshire was settled in the latter's favour. Lancaster's time had come.

Five years older than Edward, his cousin Thomas of Lancaster was 'of higher birth than the other earls'.[10] His father Edmund was the younger son of Henry III of England, his mother Blanche was the granddaughter of Louis VIII of France, his half-sister Jeanne was Philip IV's queen. To great birth was added great wealth. The Earl of Gloucester had enjoyed some £6,500 worth of land annually, but after he died at Bannockburn, leaving no issue, no other English earl held even half as much as Lancaster, whose five earldoms were worth around £11,000 a year. The value of this landed estate was enhanced by its contiguity: the great majority of what Earl Thomas held was in the north Midlands, south Yorkshire and south Lancashire, affording him the sort of virtually unchallenged domination of a cohesive territorial bloc that was very rare in England.

Allied to the crown, such power was one of a king's greatest assets. Thomas's father Edmund had been unswervingly loyal to Edward I, and initially their sons gave every sign of being good friends: they often campaigned together in Scotland between 1300 and 1307, and when Lancaster briefly fell ill in 1305, Edward wrote expressing the hope that he would soon be able to come 'to see you and comfort you'.[11] Within five years, however, affection had turned to mutual loathing, a rift which Gaveston's killing made irreparable and which would endure as long as both men drew breath.

That Edward's folly was largely to blame for this is undeniable, but contemporaries found little to admire in his cousin and even his modern biographer has commented on his 'almost repulsive' nature.[12] Violent, brooding and casuistic, Lancaster was primarily responsible for the militarization of political society which the reign witnessed, recruiting a private army to overawe his enemies and waging private wars to enforce dubious claims. At times, he would bring 2,500 armed retainers to parliaments.[13] Despite his great wealth, he never missed a chance to extort greater sums from his tenants, but still borrowed extensively to fund his extravagance and his political ambitions. Widely disliked – even by his younger brother Henry, who wanted no part in his schemes – he tried to present opposition as a duty and himself as a man of principle bent on restoring 'the dignity of the crown';[14] he even had a plaque erected in memory of the Ordinances in St Paul's Cathedral. In reality, he seems (like his cousin) to have had a limited appetite for work and to have used the Ordinances as a screen behind which to hide vindictiveness, self-interest and a dearth of constructive ideas.

This is not to deny that the Ordinances constituted a workable, in many ways commendable, programme of reform: the English episcopacy considered them to be 'a remedy for the poor and oppressed'.[15] Three years on from their publication, the original forty-one clauses had undergone a process of distillation, their perceived relevance now focusing on four or five cardinal points. Fundamental to their enforcement was the demand that the king should take major decisions only with the consent of the barons in Parliament.

In addition to war and peace policy, this included royal patronage such as grants of lands, offices, wardships, marriages and annuities – restraint of the king's prodigality being seen as the *sine qua non* of crown solvency. Since Edward had so far ignored attempts to curb his patronage, calls for restraint were now also accompanied by demands for the resumption of grants he had made during the past few years. Successful implementation of such a policy depended on the king also agreeing to two further points: that crown revenues be collected in the first place by the Exchequer, rather than being diverted to, for example, the royal household, so that central direction or at least information could be maintained over the way they were distributed; and that 'evil counsellors' be driven from court, not least because they were the prime beneficiaries of royal prodigality.

If all this were done, claimed Lancaster, the king would soon be in a position to moderate his demands for taxation, his crippling and unsanctioned *prises* of foodstuffs and other supplies, his summonses for unpaid military service and the massive loans negotiated for him by his unpopular Florentine and Genoese bankers.[16] Before 1310, the crown had relied principally on the Florentine Frescobaldi bankers for loans, but their influence was deeply resented and the Ordainers ordered the seizure of their goods; they fled England in 1311 and were bankrupted. Their place was taken by the Genoese 'financial wizard' Antonio Pessagno, who negotiated £140,000 in loans for Edward between 1312 and 1319 and was knighted for his services in 1315, although when he applied to become a freeman of the city of London his application was rejected.[17]

This was the reform programme to which Edward agreed at York in September 1314 and again at the Westminster parliament of January 1315, where the Earl of Warwick was appointed as head of the king's council. Warwick – said to have had 'no peer in wisdom and counsel'[18] – insisted like Lancaster on strict adherence to the Ordinances, and the next six months saw concerted attempts to resume royal grants, enforce Exchequer control and purge the royal household and administration. One of those obliged to retire from court was Hugh Despenser the Elder, for whom Lancaster and Warwick had an assiduously nurtured loathing. It was a time of political realignment: Hereford, released from Scottish captivity in October, now joined the king's party, as did Arundel, Warenne and leading former retainers of the Earl of Gloucester such as Bartholomew de Badlesmere and Roger Damory. It was also a time of enormous difficulty: relentless rain in late 1314 and throughout the summer of 1315 led to widespread flooding and almost entirely destroyed the harvest, driving up prices and causing famine. Around 10 per cent of the population starved to death between 1315 and 1317, not just in England but in much of northern Europe, a terrible human tragedy compounded by war and social unrest. Flocks of sheep were decimated, and wool exports, the basis of England's customs revenue, fell by 40 per cent between 1313 and 1316.[19]

Yet, if government proved a massive challenge during these years, there was nothing voluntary about Edward's surrender of power. To him, the Ordinances were anathema, an unwarrantable constraint on the proper exercise of his prerogative. Had he felt strong enough to abolish them, he would have done so, but his authority was too damaged and no help could be expected from abroad: the death of the accommodating Pope Clement V in April 1314 was followed by a two-year papal interregnum, and when Philip IV of France, latterly a supportive father-in-law, died in November 1314, he was succeeded by his son Louis X, who barely had time to establish meaningful diplomatic relations with England before he too died, in June 1316.

Meanwhile, whatever Edward tried at home turned to dust and ashes. When he held a party to mark the adjournment of Parliament in April 1315, Westminster Hall caught fire; when he went rowing in September, he nearly drowned. When he 'and his feeble council' issued an ordinance on food prices in March to try to prevent profiteering, it only encouraged hoarding and inflated prices further; the Ordainers and 'wise men of the land' would never have introduced such a measure, claimed one chronicler, and within a year it was repealed.[20] The magnificently illuminated Queen Mary Psalter, which was produced under English royal patronage around this time, attempted, through analogy with the biblical Pharaoh who commissioned Joseph to fill the granaries of Egypt, to portray Edward as a ruler concerned to save his people from famine, but no one was fooled.[21]

More representative of the king's true concerns was the lavish reburial in January 1315 of Piers Gaveston, whose embalmed and stitched-together corpse had lain at Oxford for the past two and a half years but was now wrapped in three cloths of gold costing £300 before being interred in the Dominican friary at King's Langley, which became a shrine to his memory.[22] Several earls and barons attended the ceremony, though not Lancaster or Warwick. It would be almost Warwick's last opportunity to snub the king, for by the summer he was a sick man, and in August 1315 he died. Rumours that the king had had him poisoned were probably not true, but his death was an unexpected boon for Edward and a major blow to Lancaster. With Archbishop Winchelsey having died in 1313 and Robert de Clifford and Henry Percy in 1314, Earl Thomas was left increasingly isolated in his insistence on the implementation of the Ordinances.

For the moment, however, his influence continued to grow: in August he superseded Pembroke as 'captain superior' of all English forces in the north, following which he met Edward at Lincoln to agree a strategy against Bruce. Yet hardly had a campaign been planned when it had to be abandoned, since the weather made it almost impossible to raise taxes or provisions. Instead, October found Earl Thomas having to put down a revolt in Lancashire led by one of his own knights, Adam Banaster. After an orgy of violence lasting five weeks, Banaster and his colleagues were captured and executed, but the fact that they had raised the royal standard against Lancaster in the hope of gaining the king's favour was testimony to the dysfunctional relationship between the two greatest men in England.

Meanwhile, the Scots renewed their attacks, raiding Tynedale in January 1315 and six months later besieging Carlisle, which was only saved by the heroism of Sir Andrew Harclay, Sheriff of Cumberland. Durham again paid tribute, this time a sum of £1,000 to buy immunity for two years; as the Scots swept ever deeper into England, it was increasingly to King Robert, rather than King Edward, that the people of the northern counties were paying their taxes. Not since the aftermath of the Norman Conquest had the northern English counties experienced such devastation, nor would they again until the seventeenth century. Suffering communities resorted increasingly to the payment of protection money, while those in the far north saw little option but to recognize Bruce as their lord in return for immunity. When tribute was paid, the Scots generally respected the terms, but around them society was disintegrating. Desertion, depopulation and abandonment of land north of the Humber reached epidemic proportions. Just two or three Scots had to show their faces, it was said, and a hundred Englishmen would flee. James Douglas, 'the very Devil from Hell', brought terror wherever he went.[23]

The raiding of northern England alleviated the effects of famine in Scotland, but Bruce's ambition stretched much further than this. His real aim was to secure recognition of his right to the kingship of Scotland, which was not something that Edward II was prepared to concede. The English king committed large sums of money – perhaps £20,000 a year – to maintaining garrisons in the north, and it was not always his or Lancaster's fault that the large-scale campaigns they planned failed to materialize. Edward cannot be accused of ignoring the plight of his northern subjects, but nor can he be credited with making them a priority.

It was not just in Scotland that Bruce set about dismantling English hegemony. He understood well the value of appealing to separatist sentiment elsewhere in the British Isles as a means of weakening or distracting the English and their supporters, and Ireland provided one such opportunity. From its high-water mark in the late thirteenth century, English authority in Ireland was already beginning to recede as Gaelic resistance intensified, and a common enemy made natural allies of the Scots and the Gaels. To appropriate the resources of Ireland – often used by the English as a way of keeping Scottish pretensions in check on both land and sea – was also tempting. Moreover, King Robert had an ambitious brother: Edward Bruce also coveted a crown, and on 26 May 1315, accompanied by a band of gallowglasses, he landed at Larne (Antrim) and two weeks later was proclaimed High King of Ireland.

Predictably, it was among the Gaels that he found allies, notably Donal O'Neill, King of Tyrone, who championed his royal inauguration. The Anglo-Irish, however, stood firm against him. Given that Richard de Burgh, the Red Earl of Ulster, was King Robert's father-in-law, Edward Bruce might have expected a less hostile reception, but it made little difference: the Red Earl's resistance was swept aside at Connor (Antrim) and he had to retire to Connacht. Laying siege to the great coastal stronghold of Carrickfergus before marching south, the Scots also routed a force led by Roger Mortimer of Wigmore, Lord of Trim. The expectation was that Edward Bruce would now assault Dublin, the fall of which would have put the future of the whole Anglo-Irish colony in question; instead, following an inconclusive encounter in January 1316 at Ardscull (Kildare), he returned to Ulster, where he remained for the rest of the year. As it turned out, his winter campaign of 1315–16 represented his best chance of mounting a successful challenge to English rule in Ireland, for here the ceaseless rain and famine conditions which thwarted Edward II's attempts to invade Scotland proved an ally to the English, similarly thwarting Edward Bruce's plans. However, it was only a respite.

When Parliament met at Lincoln in January 1316, England's 'empire' seemed on the point of collapse. Robert Bruce did as he wished in the north, his brother was sweeping all before him in Ireland (news of Ardscull did not arrive until February), and on 28 January, the day after Parliament was meant to assemble, the Welsh nobleman Llewellyn Bren besieged Caerphilly Castle, raising fears that Wales too was about to erupt and necessitating the despatch of a 2,000-strong force to Glamorgan. Notwithstanding all this, Lancaster did not arrive at Lincoln until 10 February, and only then could meaningful discussions begin. Earl Thomas made no secret of his belief that Edward was intent on undermining him: it was, in the phrasing of a well-trained chancery clerk, 'to remove a certain doubt which the said earl was said to have entertained about the said lord king', that the Bishop of Norwich was asked to reassure him that Edward 'bore a sincere and wholehearted goodwill towards him and the other magnates of his realm'. To prove the point, Edward publicly invited his cousin to serve as head of the council. Lancaster thanked the king and 'humbly begged that he might consider it, and answer later', but he evidently did not consider it for long, for later the same day he was sworn in to his new post. Edward promised not to take important decisions without his advice and, inevitably, to uphold the Ordinances. It was also agreed that, if the king ignored his advice, Lancaster could resign 'without ill-will, challenge, or resentment'.[24]

To all appearances, Earl Thomas had won the power he had long craved. Yet, whatever oaths were sworn or safeguards put in place, the bad blood between Edward and his cousin was by now a cancer beyond remission. The new commission set up at Lincoln to reform the government consisted largely of the king's supporters, and Lancaster simply could not work with it. Within two months, he had effectively ceased to act as head of the council, and in the summer of 1316, after a blazing row with Edward at York, he retired to his northern strongholds, ignoring summonses to councils, parliaments and even the christening of the king's second son, John, born in August. It was the end of any meaningful attempt by Lancaster to involve himself in government. For the rest of his life, he remained almost continuously on his estates in the north Midlands and Yorkshire – especially at his beloved Pontefract Castle, which he spent thousands of pounds refurbishing and fortifying – sniping and jeering but refusing to negotiate with the king except through intermediaries. Increasingly a one-man opposition, he knew that his protective shield of retainers made him immune from attack and had no compunction in using them to advance his territorial claims.

The king was helpless, for without the co-operation of the Lancastrian retinue little could be done to contain the

Scots, who in the summer of 1316 harried as far south as Swaledale and Lancashire north of the Lune, carrying off great quantities of iron from Furness, 'because Scotland is not rich in iron'.[25] In November, the king appointed the Earl of Arundel as warden of the Scottish March, superseding Lancaster's command and terminating the latter's tenure of government office. A few weeks later, the election as Bishop of Durham of Louis de Beaumont, a man whom Earl Thomas detested, marked a further diminution of his influence in the north. Yet without him it was almost impossible to organize a campaign, and instead Edward instructed Arundel to conclude a truce with the Scots.

Lancaster's withdrawal from government was not entirely unjustified: his belief, or at least his excuse, was that the 'evil counsellors' who surrounded the king were his enemies and that if he came to court they would have him arrested or killed. Given that Edward had sworn vengeance for Gaveston's death, such fears were not unfounded, but what gave Lancaster's allegations credibility was the rise to power of a new group of royal favourites. Chief among them were Hugh Despenser the Elder, now once again firmly ensconced at court; his son, Hugh the Younger; William de Montague, steward of the royal household and 'captain of the king's knights'; Roger Damory and Hugh Audley. The Elder Despenser had been unequivocally loyal since the start of the reign, but the other four had only recently risen to prominence 'in the king's shadow', an ascent almost entirely fuelled by royal patronage.[26] When the Earl of Gloucester was killed at Bannockburn, he left no issue, so that his three sisters were his co-heiresses. One of them, Eleanor, was already married to the Younger Despenser, a reward for his father's loyalty; the other two were widows, Margaret (Gaveston's former wife) and Elizabeth. Whoever now married each of them stood to inherit a third of the £6,500 Gloucester inheritance.

This was precisely the sort of great political decision which the Ordinances decreed that the king should take only with the advice of Parliament, which is doubtless why Edward had so far avoided committing himself, despite growing pressure from the Younger Despenser to proceed to partition of the lands. By early 1317, however, with Lancaster marginalized, the king felt strong enough to act, and in April Elizabeth married Roger Damory, Margaret married Hugh Audley, and the lands were valued and partitioned, instantly propelling the three husbands into the ranks of the baronage. In another delayed act of royal grace that would have been anathema to Lancaster, Edward granted the wardship of the deceased Earl of Warwick's lands to the Elder Despenser in return for £666 a year payable at the Exchequer, less than a third of their true value.

The Despensers, Damory, Audley and Montague saw themselves as a caucus: on 1 June 1317, in the king's presence at Westminster, they formally bound themselves to each other by pledges of £6,000 each. Although not specified, the purpose of these bonds was clear enough: to create a united front against Lancaster's desire to destroy them, whether by violence or by resuming their grants from the king. Their hatred of Earl Thomas was well known: at meetings of the royal council in February and April 1317, they had spoken openly of him as a traitor and a public enemy.[27] Rumour had it that they also used these meetings to plot the abduction of his wife, although it was not one of the new favourites but the Earl of Warenne (who had attended the council in February) who did the deed, carrying off Countess Alice from Canford (Dorset) on 9 May. It was said that she was abducted 'not by way of adultery, but in contempt of the earl', which was probably true, although relations between Earl Thomas and his childless wife were known to be cool and she was evidently not an unwilling victim.[28] Yet, whatever Warenne's motivation, it was an act of high folly on his part, and would cost him dear.

Lancaster, not surprisingly, saw the hand of the king and the new court clique behind the abduction, for, like almost all the earls and most of the barons, Warenne was by this time firmly in the king's camp. Starting in September 1316, Edward had made a series of indentures with leading members of the nobility, retaining them to serve him in peace and war in return for fees ranging between £100 and £1,333 a year.[29] The recipients included great men such as Pembroke and Hereford, who received the largest sums, the Younger Despenser, Amory, Audley, Montague and other barons such as Bartholomew de Badlesmere, John de Mowbray and John Giffard, who would soon have greater roles to play in the kingdom's affairs. Edward was building a coalition, the primary purpose of which may have been to deal with the Scots, but which also had the effect of binding men to him personally, with all that entailed for their future conduct. On the one hand, they each now had a vested interest in resisting Lancaster's demand for the resumption of royal grants; on the other hand, should they later oppose the king, the penalties for breach of faith would be correspondingly greater.

By now Edward was moving on to the offensive against his enemies. In August 1316 a new pope, John XXII, was finally elected, and four months later Pembroke, Badlesmere and the Bishops of Ely and Norwich were sent to find out what help he could offer Edward. Various financial concessions were agreed, but a request for the king to be absolved from his oath to the Ordinances was not, Pope John remarking that they had been drawn up by 'trustworthy persons who were unlikely to have ordained anything inimical to the kingdom or the Church'.[30] However, the main purpose of the embassy was to secure the condemnation of Robert and Edward Bruce, and in this it was successful. They were ordered under threat of excommunication to cease their attacks on England and Ireland, and two cardinal-legates were despatched to England to try to negotiate a peace. In fact, 1317 witnessed a suspension of Scottish raiding into northern England, though not in Ireland, for in January 1317 Robert Bruce crossed to Ulster and for the next three months the Bruce brothers led their joint force southwards, past Dublin – which once again anticipated a siege but was spared – as far as Cashel, then west to Limerick. Yet, despite much destruction, they gained little of long-term value and it was a depleted and half-starved Scottish army that straggled back to Ulster in May, whereupon King Robert returned home.

Almost every year of the reign thus far had seen the

planning of a royal campaign to Scotland, and 1317 was no exception. As usual, the muster was postponed from month to month, but by 4 September the king had arrived at York with the nucleus of an army. Twenty miles south, at Pontefract, Lancaster too was gathering his retainers, but with mischief makers putting it about that Edward intended to have him arrested, he was refusing to join the royalist force, claiming as usual that the king had not taken proper counsel before announcing the muster. Instead, as soon as he heard that Edward was at York, he provocatively posted troops on the bridges over the Aire and the Wharfe to prevent reinforcements from joining him. It was a moment of great tension, further heightened by the kidnapping near Darlington of Louis de Beaumont, who was on his way to be consecrated as Bishop of Durham, and the two cardinal-legates sent by Pope John to negotiate an Anglo-Scottish peace. Given his well-known antipathy to Beaumont, Lancaster was immediately suspected of complicity, although in fact he acted quickly to secure the cardinals' release.

Once again, however, the relationship between the king and his cousin found new depths to plumb. Aborting the Scottish campaign, Edward retraced his steps and, as he approached Pontefract, arrayed his forces for battle. Damory and others urged him to attack, but fortunately Pembroke persuaded Edward not to embark on a course that would surely lead to civil war. Relenting, the king resumed his journey, while Lancaster and his men lined the walls and embankments to jeer them on their way. No sooner had Edward gone south than Earl Thomas sent his retainers to seize Knaresborough Castle, which was held by Damory, and devastate Warenne's lands in Yorkshire, including his castles of Sandal and Conisborough.[31] Only by using overwhelming force, Lancaster had evidently concluded, could he take his revenge on the hated favourites.

'Whatever the lord king wants, the earl's servants try to upset, and whatever the earl wants, the king's servants call treachery,' lamented the author of the *Vita*.[32] It was at this point, however, that the cardinal-legates stumbled upon their true mission – not to make peace between the English and the Scots, but between Edward and Lancaster. For the next ten months, while Earl Thomas skulked in his Midland and Yorkshire castles, they shuttled almost ceaselessly, accompanied by a fluid grouping of English bishops, between the king and his cousin, trying to find a basis for agreement. In the midst of this, in early April 1318, came the news that the English had long dreaded, the capture by the Scots of that great bastion of the East March, Berwick-on-Tweed. Berwick was the hub of the lucrative borders wool trade; after Edward I captured it in 1296, it became the headquarters of his northern administration. The Scots made at least five attempts to retake it, and in 1312 it was saved only when the barking of a dog alerted the townspeople to the danger. Eventually, however, on the night of 1 April 1318, a watchman was bribed by James Douglas to allow a party of Scots to scale the walls. The English burgesses were expelled and replaced by Scots, and this time, rather than demolishing the fortifications, Robert Bruce heightened and strengthened them. It was a sign of his growing pretensions, and Douglas followed it up with a pitiless raid as far south as Wharfedale and Airedale before turning west and following the valley of the Ribble to Preston. Ripon and its minster were spared in return for £666, but Northallerton, Boroughbridge, Knaresborough, Skipton-in-Craven and 'all the parishes of Lancaster' were wasted or burned.[33] Earl Thomas's lands were spared, however, and the rumours that he was colluding with Bruce now became deafening.

By now, the Scottish king controlled roughly one-fifth of England, from which he was raising tribute of some £5,000 a year, and Edward knew that if he did not act soon it might be too late. A few days after Berwick's fall, therefore, Pembroke, Badlesmere and a group of prelates met once more with Lancaster, this time at Leicester, and a draft agreement was drawn up. The main issues to be settled were the resumption of royal grants and the penalties to be incurred by the favourites who had profited from the king's prodigality. Although Edward desperately needed Lancaster's help against Bruce, he was also under intense pressure from the courtiers not to deprive them or allow them to suffer punishment. On this point, however, Lancaster was insistent: Damory and Montague, who had plotted to kill him, and Warenne, the abductor of his wife, must pay him reparations and be banished from court. Further tortuous negotiations followed in June, and by July, with Edward now based at Northampton and Earl Thomas at Tutbury, mediators were passing between them weekly. It resembled international diplomacy – a measure of Lancaster's power.

Eventually, once the king had given written guarantees

for the safety of Lancaster and his followers, a meeting was arranged and articles drawn up. The cousins met at Leake (Nottinghamshire) on 9 August 1318, where they 'spoke long and intimately', exchanged the kiss of peace, dined together, and sealed the agreement; as a sign of his 'abundance of love' for his cousin, the king gave Lancaster a palfrey.[34] The Treaty of Leake set up a council to monitor the king and promised unconditional pardons to Lancaster and his supporters; it also confirmed the Ordinances. In return, Earl Thomas agreed to set aside his enmity against all except Warenne: even Damory, Audley and Montague, having promised to pay him reparations totalling £1,700, were received into his grace. This was doubtless why there was no mention of retribution against them, nor even of resumption, although in fact Montague was replaced as steward of the king's household by Badlesmere in October, and he, Damory and Audley were much less frequently at court from now onwards. Warenne, however, found no forgiveness and was effectively abandoned by Edward, who declared that his quarrel with Lancaster was a private matter. Two months after Leake, he was made to suffer for his recklessness when Lancaster forced him to hand over all his lands in Yorkshire and pay him the impossible sum of £50,000; according to Warenne, Lancaster threatened to put him to death if he did not comply.

Yet, if Warenne was the loser, the prevailing mood in the autumn of 1318 was one of optimism, and when in October the severed head of Edward Bruce arrived, a gift to the king from the jubilant Anglo-Irish who had effectively ended the Scottish invasion of Ireland by massacring him and his army at Faughart (County Louth), it became almost euphoric. 'Great hope has latterly grown up in us,' declared the author of the *Vita* in the winter of 1318–19, 'because God has gladdened king and people with many signs of prosperity.' Firstly, the pope had excommunicated Robert Bruce and laid Scotland under interdict; secondly, Edward Bruce had been killed; thirdly, the rain had at last ceased, prices had fallen, and famine had been relieved; fourthly, 'our king has been reconciled to his barons. Now, forsaking frivolities, he listens to their advice, and there is no longer anyone to lead him astray, for the clique that opposed the barons has now left the court.'[35] One man who had not left court, however, was Hugh Despenser the Younger. Distracted perhaps by his loathing for the Elder Hugh, Lancaster seems to have overlooked the steady rise to favour in 1316–17 of his son, which was crowned by his appointment in the summer of 1318 as the king's chamberlain, leaving him deftly positioned to step into the vacuum created by the departure of Damory, Montague and Audley.

3
'The King's Right Eye'

At the beginning of July 1318, with the negotiations with Lancaster at their most tense, a man called John of Powderham, the son of a tanner from Exeter, was brought before the king at Northampton after claiming that he, not Edward II, was the true King of England. Edward, he insisted, was really the son of a groom or a carter, a changeling smuggled into the royal nursery following an accident. At first Edward refused to take him seriously. 'Welcome, my brother!' he jeered when John first appeared before him, suggesting that he be given a wand and put to work as a jester, but Queen Isabella and others, more alert to the danger, realized that if the rumour spread it could seriously damage the king's credibility. A formal trial was thus held in the royal household, presided over by William Montague as steward. John's parents were summoned from Exeter to confirm his birth, and notwithstanding his plea that he had been misled by the Devil, he was drawn and hanged.[1]

Despite the delicacy of the political situation, there was no suggestion that he had been put up to this by Lancaster or anyone else. What made his allegations dangerous was Edward's unkingly behaviour – rowing, carting, grooming horses – evidence to a society with a strong belief in heredity of unkingly blood. News of the impostor spread and, 'because the said Edward resembled the elder Edward in none of his virtues', was apparently widely believed. It was a measure of how low the king's reputation had sunk. There was still hope, however: as the author of the *Vita* pointed out, the great Nebuchadnezzar achieved 'nothing memorable' during the first twelve years of his reign, but after that 'he began to flourish and to conquer nations and kingdoms'; would that Edward might emulate him, and 'now at least try to attack his enemies, so that he might repair the damage and disgrace which he has borne so long'.[2] And at first the omens were good. At the York parliament of October 1318 – the first that Lancaster had attended for nearly three years – the Treaty of Leake and the Ordinances were confirmed, a review of royal grants was instituted, and a schedule drawn up for the reform of the king's household. Even after Edward returned to Westminster early in 1319, he continued to acknowledge the authority of the standing council set up at Leake.

The main business during the spring of 1319 was to plan a Scottish campaign. In May, another parliament at York granted taxes, and by early August a force of some 10,000 infantry and 500 cavalry had mustered at Newcastle, while around 80 ships were requisitioned to ferry supplies up the coast. It was the most impressive English military effort for five years and the most unified of the reign: for the first time since 1307, even Lancaster agreed to serve, providing about one-fifth of the royal army. The first objective was Berwick, which was reached on

7 September and stormed the next day, though without success. A second assault on 13 September almost succeeded, but at this point things began to go wrong.

Barely had the king arrived at Berwick when he began, 'with his usual fatuity', to court controversy by handing out favours: once it was captured, he is alleged to have declared, he would make Damory captain of the town, the Younger Despenser captain of the castle, and finally get his revenge for Gaveston's death.[3] The mood in the besiegers' camp was thus already fragile when, on the morning of 14 September, news arrived of another Scottish incursion. Led by Randolph and Douglas, a diversionary force had crossed the border at the end of August and, avoiding Edward's army, pressed on to Myton-on-Swale, near York, where on 12 September it annihilated a makeshift home guard led by the archbishop and mayor of York. Because of the large number of clerics killed, the engagement came to be known as the Chapter of Myton. The only compensation was that the Scots had failed in their attempt to seize Queen Isabella, whom Edward had left at York, but the debacle threw the continuance of the siege of Berwick into the balance. As soon as the news arrived, the king held a council: he and the southern lords were for pressing on with the siege, but Lancaster and some of the northerners claimed that they needed to go home to protect their lands, and three days later Lancaster left, taking his two thousand or so retainers with him. Without them, it was impossible to continue the siege, and by 21 September Edward and the remnants of his army were back at Newcastle, while Randolph and Douglas ravaged their way back to Scotland via the West March. Yet another English campaign had collapsed in ignominy, and the north was desperate for a respite. In December 1319 a two-year Anglo-Scottish truce was agreed.

The political settlement of 1318–19 now started to unravel in a welter of recrimination. Rumours abounded concerning Lancaster's 'treachery' at Berwick: that he had received £40,000 from Bruce to subvert the siege; that he had passed unhindered through James Douglas's lines and Douglas through his. The man Lancaster blamed for spreading these tales was the Younger Despenser, and not without reason, for a letter written by Despenser on 21 September to his chief agent in Wales, John Inge, put the blame for the raising of the siege squarely on Earl Thomas and alleged that the Scottish invasion had been undertaken with his 'encouragement and assistance'. Whatever the truth of the matter in 1319, within another two years at most it had become clear that Lancaster was colluding with Bruce.[4]

By this time a new clique of favourites was establishing a stranglehold on the king's favour. Montague died in 1319, Damory and Audley were rapidly losing ground, and although Pembroke was still at court he was by now an elder statesman enjoying little real power. The Elder Despenser, however, trading on his son's new-found prominence, was once more firmly embedded in the king's inner circle, as were Bartholomew de Badlesmere, who had replaced Montague as steward of the royal household, and Robert Baldock, appointed in January 1320 as keeper of the king's privy seal. Head and shoulders above them all, however, was the Younger Despenser.

Hugh Despenser the Younger was the king's junior by two years, and to many his rise seemed all too reminiscent of the Gaveston years, but the two favourites were quite different men. Where Gaveston was charming and foolish, Despenser was a clever and manipulative bully. Unlike Gaveston, he had not risen 'as if from nothing'. His father, Hugh the Elder, had served Edward I and Edward II as soldier, diplomat and councillor with conspicuous loyalty for twenty-five years, trusted by both kings to the same degree as he was distrusted by their opponents. Almost alone among the barons, he had supported Gaveston to the end and refused to put his seal to the Ordinances.[5] That is why Lancaster hated him and why he was obliged to withdraw from court in 1318. Meanwhile, his son was steadily, almost stealthily, worming his way into royal favour, and by 1320, with Damory and Audley shuffled off to the wings, the stage was set for him to exploit to the full his appointment as Edward's chamberlain.

The chamberlainship was a post of great influence – or at least it had the potential to be, for the chamberlain controlled access to the royal apartments, vetting suitors and intercessors and deciding who should or should not be admitted to the king's presence. Contemporaries were in no doubt that the Younger Despenser took full advantage of the opportunities it afforded: 'If anyone wished to speak with the king, he did not dare to do so except in the presence of Sir Hugh'; he was 'not just a second king, but the ruler of the king, and he had bewitched the king's mind'; 'his commandments were carried out everywhere and in every way, and everyone feared and hated him from the bottom of their hearts'.[6] He was, concluded one, 'the king's right eye'.[7] Handsome, haughty and inordinately greedy, Hugh was later accused of being a sodomite, but it may be that it was his wife, Eleanor de Clare, the king's niece, whom Edward loved; the king certainly showed great fondness for her, and there were rumours that she was his mistress.[8] Despenser himself seems to have been almost as much feared as loved by Edward, but the king also found his financial acumen indispensable. He told the king that he would make him wealthy and spared no effort to see that he did; what Hugh really wanted, though, as he wrote to John Inge, was that 'Despenser may be rich and may attain his ends, of which Inge is well aware'.[9] Even when writing to his most trusted officials, his letters exuded an air of menace. It was not so much outrage, as with Gaveston, that motivated the opposition to Despenser, but real fear.

A third of the earldom of Gloucester would have satisfied many a baron, but not the Younger Despenser. His share of the Clare inheritance consisted principally of the lordship of Glamorgan with its great castles at Cardiff and Caerphilly, but no sooner had the partition been agreed in November 1317 than he began scheming to enlarge it. In March 1318 he was told to keep his hands off Newport, which bordered Glamorgan to the east and had been apportioned to Hugh Audley, but he ignored the order and by the end of the year had pressurized Audley into ceding it in return for less valuable lands in England. To the west of Glamorgan lay Dryslwyn and Cantref Mawr, over which he persuaded the king to grant him control, and he made no secret of the fact that he also coveted Cantref

Bychan and Brecon to the north, which were held by John Giffard of Brimpsfield and Roger Mortimer of Chirk respectively. Following the death of the dowager countess of Gloucester, he also set his sights on the lordship of Usk, even though by right it fell to Roger Damory. His aim was nothing less than to reconstitute the earldom of Gloucester, and it was widely believed that before long the title would be his as well.

Damory, Audley, Mortimer and Giffard were men who had served Edward II loyally, but as it became increasingly clear that the king was prepared to connive at Despenser's self-aggrandizement, their loyalty disintegrated. During the early months of 1320, the king was preoccupied with Anglo-French affairs, for Philip V, who had succeeded his brother Louis X as King of France in 1316, had been pressing for some time for the English king to do homage for Gascony. On 19 June, therefore, Edward crossed the Channel, performing homage to Philip at Amiens Cathedral on 30 June and not returning to London until 2 August. It was after his return, said the author of the *Vita*, that 'a great quarrel arose between some of the greater barons and Hugh Despenser the son'.[10] At its heart lay the lordship of Gower, centred on Swansea, held by the elderly Marcher baron William de Braose. Braose's only son had died in 1315, and although he had designated his son-in-law John de Mowbray as his heir, with reversion to the Earl of Hereford, the Younger Despenser spied an opportunity. Barely had Mowbray entered upon his inheritance when, on 26 October 1320, Despenser persuaded the king not to sanction the alienation and instead to seize

Gower, probably on the grounds that no royal licence had been issued for its alienation.

The latter was true, but whether the king was entitled to intervene was debatable. The Marcher lordships, into which east and south Wales was partitioned, had been created piecemeal during the twelfth and thirteenth centuries as a kind of buffer zone between England and the native Welsh principalities, and their lords' 'service' to the crown consisted in effect in the subjection of the Welsh and the protection of the border. In return, they enjoyed a range of judicial, financial and administrative privileges such as the right to make private war and to exchange or alienate lands without royal permission. Although these did not always go unchallenged by the crown, especially since the king now held north-western Wales, Edward's disregard for the Marchers' privileges in the interests of his favourite united them against him.[11] The Younger Despenser, they now saw, was a threat to all of them, and they were determined to resist him; the problem was that they would also have to resist the king.

Contemporaries began to notice a change in Edward's behaviour around this time. During the October 1320 parliament – so the Bishop of Worcester informed the pope – the king was getting up earlier than usual, attending almost every day and taking a constructive interest in the business of the realm. A chronicler noted that, 'to the amazement of many', Edward 'showed prudence in answering the petitions of the poor, and as much clemency as severity in judicial matters'. When he met Philip V at Amiens in the summer, he agreed to pay homage for

Gascony, but when also asked to swear fealty he vigorously asserted that this had not been demanded of previous English kings and 'we certainly do not intend to do so'.[12] Stunned into silence, the French dropped the matter. Galvanized perhaps by the Younger Despenser, Edward was demonstrating that he was no longer willing to be pushed around, a robustness that also manifested itself in his dealings with Lancaster. Well aware that Earl Thomas loathed every one of them, the king and his tight little circle of favourites now abandoned their attempts to reconcile him, leaving him to glower ineffectually from Pontefract. For the moment, the fact that he continued to treat the north like a private fiefdom mattered less, for the Anglo-Scottish truce had relieved the pressure. The truce also reduced the king's demands for men, money and provisions from his subjects, boosting both his personal standing and the economic recovery which had followed the good harvests of 1318, 1319 and 1320. Optimism was to be short-lived, however: to be sure, kingly vigour was a quality to be admired, but it could also be manipulated, and no one knew how to do so better than the Younger Despenser.

In November 1320, there were signs that the king was still looking to compromise: financial inducements were offered to some of the disaffected, and the partition of the Gloucester inheritance was confirmed. In December, however, royal officials took possession of Gower, making it clear that the threat to the Marchers had not been lifted, and early in 1321 the latter began organizing for war, withdrawing to their lordships, leaguing together and summoning their retainers. Their spokesman was Humphrey, Earl of

Hereford, a royalist since 1314 and the widower of the king's favourite sister, Elizabeth, but now enraged by Edward's refusal to acknowledge his concerns. Earl Humphrey also bore a private grudge against the Younger Despenser, who had executed the Welsh rebel Llewellyn Bren in barbarous fashion after Hereford had accepted his surrender. Behind him ranged most of the barons of the southern and middle March – John de Mowbray, John Giffard of Brimpsfield, the erstwhile favourites Damory and Audley, Roger Mortimer of Chirk and his nephew and namesake of Wigmore – who, according to the author of the *Vita*, 'unanimously decided that Hugh Despenser [the Younger] must be pursued, brought down and utterly destroyed'. When Despenser's tenants approached them to offer support, they were informed that they must renounce their allegiance to Despenser and agree never to acknowledge him as their lord.[13] When Edward invited Hereford to a council to discuss his grievances, Earl Humphrey refused to appear until Hugh was removed from the king's presence. Ominously, the Marchers were also in contact with Lancaster, who made no secret of his support for them despite his reluctance to join them in taking action.

Although it was the Marchers who set the pace in 1321 – not least because private warfare was an accepted way to settle differences in the March – opposition to the Younger Despenser also ran deep within the royal circle. During the earlier crises of 1308–12 and 1316–18, the knights of the household, of whom there were usually fifty to sixty, remained overwhelmingly loyal, but by 1321 many of them had either left or been dismissed from the king's service and no fewer than twenty-five of them later joined the opposition. So too did twenty-four barons, most of whom were not Marchers: they included Maurice de Berkeley and Roger de Clifford. Supremely confident of the king's support, Despenser had no qualms about targeting the strong along with the less strong. He manipulated the law to his own and his retainers' advantage, monopolized royal patronage and filled the royal household with placemen such as Robert Baldock. Edward, apparently oblivious to the danger of allowing the royal retinue, the bedrock of his personal and military support, to fragment in such fashion, denounced those who opposed him as 'Contrariants'; like the Marchers, many of them were undeniably threatened by the insatiable favourite, but they were also trying to save the king from the consequences of his own folly.[14]

Warned by his ubiquitous spies that an attack on the Younger Despenser's lands was imminent, Edward left Windsor on 6 March 1321 and by the end of the month had reached Gloucester, where he ordered the seizure of some of Damory's and Audley's castles. Hereford now wrote to the king suggesting that the Younger Despenser should be committed to Lancaster's keeping until he could be brought before Parliament, but Edward was never going to agree to that. He replied (rather deftly) that his chamberlain had not technically been accused of any crime and that to place him in custody would contravene both Magna Carta and the Ordinances; if Hereford wanted a parliament, why would he not come to a council to set a date for one? By this time, however, the Contrariants, 'white-hot with hatred', were mobilized for war, and probably the only thing that could have prevented it was the banishment of the Despensers, which the king continued to resist.[15]

The threatened violence erupted at the beginning of May. The first of the Younger Despenser's lands to be targeted was Newport Castle, which was assaulted on 4 May. Its capitulation four days later was followed by the systematic devastation of his properties, causing damage later estimated at £14,000, and the capture of Cardiff and Swansea on 9 and 13 May respectively. Resistance was minimal, since neither the Welsh nor the English had any desire to fight for the hated favourite. Nor did Despenser's allies escape: Roger Mortimer of Wigmore attacked Clun, a lordship held by the Earl of Arundel, who in February had married his son to Hugh's daughter. A few of the Elder Despenser's properties in Wiltshire were also raided, but an attempt to win over the citizens of Bristol failed when the mayor declared his loyalty to the king. Nevertheless, by early June the aggrieved Marchers had regained control of the lordships they claimed, while the king, 'with his own Hugh always at his side', had withdrawn to London.[16]

The outbreak of hostilities was the cue for Lancaster to enter the fray. For the first time in five years, Earl Thomas was presented with the opportunity to move from one-man opposition to leadership of a party, and although he did not for the moment wish to join in the raids on the Despensers' lands, he wanted to ensure in so far as he could that his own agenda was not ignored. Whereas the Contrariants' wrath was focused on the Younger Despenser, Lancaster regarded his father as equally culpable and impressed upon his new-found allies that both of them must be removed.[17]

As was his wont, he had also developed an intense loathing for Bartholomew de Badlesmere, perhaps because he felt that, being the hereditary steward of England – a point he seldom failed to mention in his dealings with Edward – he should have had the right to appoint the steward of the royal household. Although Lancaster still took his stand on the Ordinances, in practice his 'programme', such as it was, had by now boiled down to the removal of the 'evil counsellors' who surrounded the king, the grievance most likely to attract the widest support. Yet he also needed to ensure that support within his heartland remained solid, for by now some of his own retainers were getting nervous about where Earl Thomas's persistent defiance of the king might lead them, and desertions from his retinue were mounting.

It was to try to satisfy these various needs that Lancaster twice summoned what some contemporaries termed parliaments, the first at Pontefract on 24 May 1321, the second at Sherburn-in-Elmet, eight miles north of Pontefract, on 28 June. His aim was to build a coalition strong enough to force the king to do his bidding, to which end he summoned some fifteen lords from the northern counties as well as his own retainers and the leading Contrariants. The Bishops of York, Durham and Carlisle also attended, perhaps in the hope that they could act as intermediaries. His 'parliaments' certainly did not give Lancaster everything he wanted, for the northern lords and bishops, fearful of the consequences of rebellion, refused to commit themselves. However, the southern Contrariants seemed happy to accept his leadership, not least because of the legitimacy his tenure of the stewardship conferred on their actions, and he probably went some way towards reassuring his more hesitant retainers.

There was also one unexpected conversion to the opposition. Warned in advance about the Sherburn meeting, the king sent the Archbishop of Canterbury and Bartholomew de Badlesmere to try to persuade the barons to desist from violence and bring their grievances to a real parliament, but to Edward's surprise and fury Badlesmere promptly changed sides. The king's steward had close connections with several of the leading rebels, but his overriding reason for joining them was almost certainly jealousy of the Younger Despenser, who by this time had eclipsed him at court and was probably instrumental in securing his removal from the constableship of Dover Castle five days before the Sherburn assembly. Needless to say, Badlesmere immediately lost the stewardship as well. Yet if he thought that by switching sides he could allay Earl Thomas's enmity towards him, he was mistaken. Lancaster had never located a burial ground for hatchets, and in the long term Badlesmere's defection weakened rather than strengthened the baronial coalition, introducing internal divisions and mutual distrust. As with the opposition to Gaveston, this was a coalition united by little more than the desire to remove a royal favourite.

For the moment, however, its objective was clear and its resolve undimmed. Edward, taken aback by the strength of the opposition, tried to rally support by summoning a parliament to Westminster on 15 July. Mindful of what had happened to Gaveston, he also placed the Despensers out of

1. Edward II's alabaster tomb effigy in the north ambulatory of Gloucester Cathedral. The chronicler Ranulf Higden described the king as 'a handsome man of great strength, but unconventional in his behaviour'.

2. Edward I invests his son as Prince of Wales in February 1301. The young Edward was the first heir to the throne to bear this title, symbolic of his father's ambitions in the British Isles.

3. Edward II's marriage to Isabella, daughter of King Philip IV of France, at Boulogne, 25 January 1308. He was twenty-three, she was twelve.

4. *Edward II and Gaveston*, by the Pre-Raphaelite painter Marcus Stone, first exhibited at the Royal Academy in 1872.

5. This late fifteenth-century illustration by the chronicler John Rous shows Guy, Earl of Warwick, trampling the decapitated Piers Gaveston, whose death in June 1312 he was instrumental in procuring.

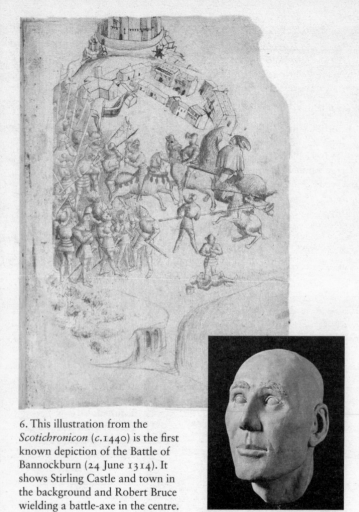

6. This illustration from the *Scotichronicon* (*c.*1440) is the first known depiction of the Battle of Bannockburn (24 June 1314). It shows Stirling Castle and town in the background and Robert Bruce wielding a battle-axe in the centre.

7. Reconstruction of the head of Robert Bruce, based on a cast of his skull, made by Brian Hill in 1996.

8. The execution of Thomas, Earl of Lancaster (22 March 1322). 'This earl, lately the terror of the whole land,' wrote a chronicler, 'stretched forth his neck as if in prayer, and with two or three blows the executioner cut off his head.'

9. This French manuscript illustration depicts Queen Isabella presenting the twelve-year-old Prince Edward to perform homage to King Charles IV of France at Vincennes (24 September 1325).

10. The execution of the Younger Despenser at Hereford (24 November 1326). Bound to a ladder fifty feet high, he was castrated and disembowelled before being beheaded and quartered.

11. Queen Isabella and Roger Mortimer with their army at Hereford on the day of the execution of the Younger Despenser.

12. The cell at Berkeley Castle in which Edward II is said to have been imprisoned in the summer of 1327 and murdered on 21 September.

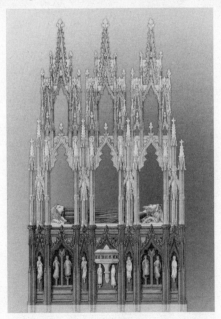

13. Reconstruction by Gemma Bryant of Edward II's effigy and tomb in Gloucester Cathedral, showing the presumed original paintwork and gold leaf on the canopy.

The troublesome

raigne and lamentable death of
Edward the second, King of
England: with the tragicall
fall of proud Mortimer:

And also the life and death of Peirs Gaueston,
the great Earle of Cornewall, and mighty
fauorite of king Edward the second, as it was
publiquely acted by the right honorable
the Earle of Pembrooke his
seruantes,

Written by Chri. Marlow Gent.

Imprinted at London by Richard Bradocke,
for William Iones dwelling neere Hosbourne conduit,
at the signe of the Gunne, 1 5 9 8,

14. Title-page to the second (1598) edition of *Edward II* by Christopher Marlowe, whose unambiguous portrayal of the king as homosexual greatly influenced subsequent accounts of his reign.

STEVEN WADDINGTON ANDREW TIERNAN TILDA SWINTON

UN FILM DE **DEREK JARMAN**

EDWARD II

D'APRÈS LA PIÈCE DE CHRISTOPHER MARLOWE

15. Poster for Derek Jarman's flamboyantly homoerotic cinematic adaptation of Marlowe's play, which reclaimed the king as a gay icon for the late twentieth century.

harm's way, entrusting Hugh the Younger to the protection of the men of the Cinque Ports. The Contrariants, after plundering Despenser properties in Leicestershire, reached the outskirts of London on 29 July, led by Hereford, the Mortimers, Damory and Audley, and accompanied by some five thousand retainers, all clothed in livery of green with yellow and white bends in the right quarter, as a result of which the meeting came to be known as 'the parliament of the white bend'.[18] Lancaster was not with them, but the king knew full well that he was behind them, and it was at Lancaster's Inn outside the capital that Hereford billeted his men. There was a last-minute attempt at mediation by the bishops, but when Badlesmere told them that the Younger Despenser was 'a manifest traitor and enemy of the king and kingdom', it was clear that the time for compromise was past.[19] Several of the prelates, the Earls of Pembroke, Arundel, Richmond and Warenne, and even Queen Isabella, now urged the king to give way in order to prevent civil war. If the Despensers were not exiled, Pembroke warned him, it was quite likely that he would lose his throne.

Backed into a corner, Edward finally submitted. Since the Despensers were absent, there was no trial and no opportunity for them to defend themselves: they were exiled by 'award' – that is, on the record – of the peers of the realm, the charges against them being read out in Westminster Hall on 14 August by Hereford. The Three Articles of 1308, originally composed to secure the exile of Gaveston, were once again presented as a way of justifying opposition to the 'unreasonable' king while maintaining faith with the crown. It was clear from the indictment that the Younger Despenser was viewed as the real culprit. It was he who had 'drawn over to his cause' his father, so that together they had usurped royal power and plotted to have 'sole government of the realm'. One of the charges against him recited how, when Edward showed reluctance to do his bidding, he 'was angry with the king' and schemed 'to lead the king to do his will by duress, with the result that he did not forgive him when he did not do it' – a revealing insight into their relationship. Charges relating to the seizure of lands in the March and the execution of Llewellyn Bren were also included, but the main thrust of the indictment was in line with the comments of the chroniclers, namely that the Despensers had monopolized access to Edward, his counsel and his patronage, thereby inciting war and imperilling the kingdom.[20]

After hearing Hereford out, Edward agreed, 'with bitterness in his soul', that both father and son should be exiled from the realm in perpetuity and their heirs disinherited; they were to leave from Dover within two weeks, and if they ever returned they would be treated as enemies of the king and the realm. All those involved in the attacks on them and their lands over the previous few months were granted statutory pardons by the king. 'Anxious and sad', Edward retired to his chamber, but two days later, while dining with the strongly royalist Bishop of Rochester, he told him that 'he would within half a year set matters to right in such a way that the entire world would take note and would tremble'.[21]

The next half-year would indeed be Edward's finest hour, and if the whole world did not tremble, England certainly did. The exile of the Despensers instantly tilted the balance of right and wrong back in favour of the king, putting the Contrariants in an almost impossible position. If they disarmed and went home, it was virtually certain that Edward would claim duress, recall the Despensers and start picking off his enemies one by one. If, however, having achieved their stated aim of saving the king and the kingdom from the hated favourites, they remained in arms, it would be the king they were opposing, laying them open to the charge of treason. Moreover, although they knew that Lancaster supported them, he showed no sign of leaving Pontefract. Not surprisingly, many of the less committed or less threatened now began to melt away, although the leading Marchers and others too deeply implicated, such as Badlesmere, remained at Oxford, ready to act if necessary.

Unslaked for a decade, Edward's thirst for vengeance would wait no longer. Just as galling to him as the Despensers' exile – as it had been during the Gaveston years – was the insult to his royal dignity, and he planned to recall them as soon as possible. He was certainly in touch with the Younger Despenser in September 1321, for although Hugh had put to sea he had not departed the realm, but was roaming the Channel and the North Sea with men of the Cinque Ports, committing acts of piracy 'like a monster of the sea' and occasionally coming ashore.[22] It was at one of his ports of call, probably Minster-in-Thanet, in early September that he and Edward met and plotted their revenge. Yet the campaign the king subsequently launched was undertaken under his personal direction; apart from a brief rendezvous at Portchester in October, he saw neither of the Despensers again until early March 1322. In the meantime, he relied on his own leadership, on his household knights and bannerets, whose ranks he hastily replenished to replace those whose reliability was suspect, and on the retinues of the Earls of Pembroke, Arundel, Warenne and Richmond, and of his half-brothers, Thomas, Earl of Norfolk and Edmund, Earl of Kent, now twenty-one and twenty respectively.

The campaign to restore royal authority was carefully planned. Back at Westminster by 25 September, Edward began by ordering the Marchers to give up the lands they had seized from the Despensers. When this was predictably ignored, he sent Queen Isabella to demand entry to Leeds Castle in Kent, which was in Badlesmere's custody, although he was not there at the time. Fearing a ruse, and under orders from Badlesmere to defend the castle, the garrison refused to admit her, whereupon, on 16 October, Edward announced his intention to besiege it. The former steward was a well-chosen target: despised by both the king and Lancaster, he was doubly vulnerable. Led by Hereford and the Mortimers, the Contrariants, when they heard of developments at Leeds, exhibited enough solidarity to advance as far as Kingston-upon-Thames (Surrey), but here they received a warning from Lancaster not to help Badlesmere since he could not be trusted. Leeds duly surrendered on 31 October, Badlesmere's wife and children were sent to the Tower of London, and thirteen of the garrison were hanged, which 'terrified everyone immensely'.[23]

November was spent preparing for war. By this time, with the number of desertions from his retinue rising, Lancaster was trying to negotiate help from the Scots, under the pseudonym 'King Arthur'. Yet the core of the Marchers' support remained solid, and by early December they had established their base at Gloucester to prevent the king from crossing the Severn and entering Wales. For the moment, Edward remained in London, where, on 1 December, a council of prelates, earls and royal justices proclaimed the exile of the Despensers to have been unlawful and authorized the despatch of safe-conducts to them. Thus fortified, Edward felt strong enough to begin operations, and having ordered his forces to muster at Cirencester, he joined them there for Christmas, pausing only to seize and destroy a number of rebel castles along the way.

On 27 December the king and his army marched out. With the crossing at Gloucester blocked, they went north to Worcester, only to find that this was also in rebel hands. An advance guard was sent to hold Bridgnorth, but on 5 January the Contrariants burned the bridge there too, so that the royal army was eventually forced to go as far north as Shrewsbury to cross the Severn. Meanwhile the king had written to his Welsh supporters to close in from the north, rightly reckoning that they would jump at the chance of vengeance against the Marchers who lorded it over them; and, once Edward entered Wales on 14 January, resistance soon crumbled. The two Roger Mortimers, whose lands in the northern and middle March were being harried by a Welsh force under Sir Griffith Lloyd, Sheriff of Merioneth and the king's key agent in north Wales, cut their losses and submitted to the king at Shrewsbury on 22 January.[24] They were sent to the Tower of London. Further defections followed as the king turned southwards: Maurice de Berkeley surrendered at Gloucester on 6 February, and even Hereford thought of giving himself up, although when he realized that the king was in no mood to grant pardons he instead fled to join Lancaster. Damory, Audley and others went with him, hastened on their way by the hanging of three rebel knights at Gloucester.

Edward's shrewd and ruthless campaign against the Contrariants had been totally successful, and all that was left to the fugitives was to put their faith in Lancaster. Had Earl Thomas come to their aid, it might have been a different story, but failure of nerve seems to have prevented him from abandoning the safety of his northern heartland. Instead, his chosen method of showing solidarity with his allies was to try (unsuccessfully) to capture the royal castle of Tickhill, twenty-five miles from Pontefract. On 8 February the king wrote to his cousin ordering him not to give any succour to the rebels; supercilious to the last, Lancaster replied that he was unaware of having encountered any, but if he did so he would be sure to kill or exile them. By now, however, his braggadocio was almost played out. Fearing that the earl would try to reach Scotland, the king ordered Sir Andrew Harclay, Sheriff of Cumberland, to cut him off, while Edward himself summoned 12,000 more men to join him at Coventry and began moving northwards, seizing Lancaster's castle of Kenilworth on the way. The net was closing, and to make matters worse for Lancaster the Archbishop of York sent the king recently discovered treasonable correspondence between him and the Scots, which Edward published on 1 March. Two days later the Despensers rejoined the king at Lichfield, and on 11 March Lancaster,

Hereford and their remaining allies were publicly denounced as traitors. Even Earl Thomas's closest lieutenants such as Sir Robert Holand, 'whom he trusted more than any man alive', now began to desert him.[25]

After trying unsuccessfully to defend the bridge at Burton-on-Trent, most of the Contrariants who had not fled now sought refuge in Pontefract Castle. Others went into hiding, though not Damory, who had been mortally wounded at Burton and left behind at Tutbury, where the king caught up with him on 13 March. Although convicted of treason, the former favourite was spared public execution and allowed to die of his wounds in the abbey. Meanwhile, at Pontefract, confusion reigned. Lancaster, still under the illusion that Edward might accept that they had taken up arms not against him but against the Despensers, and perhaps believing that the king would not dare to put his own cousin to death, thought they should hold out and hope for terms. Others thought they should throw themselves on Edward's mercy, but the majority opinion was that they should flee to the Lancastrian stronghold of Dunstanburgh in Northumberland and hope that the king's anger might cool. Only when Roger de Clifford drew his sword on him did Lancaster agree to go with them. However, they got no further than Boroughbridge, where they found Andrew Harclay guarding the bridge over the Ure with 4,000 northerners, all dismounted and packed into schiltrons bristling with pikes and longbows, 'according to the manner of the Scots'.[26] Desperation spurred the Contrariant army forward. Hereford led an assault to try to force a crossing but was killed by a

Welshman lurking below, who found 'a hole in the planking and stabbed him in the groin, a private part where soldiers are not usually protected'.[27] Following this, hostilities were suspended for the night, but early the next morning, 17 March, Harclay's men surrounded the Contrariant camp. Lancaster tried to slip away in disguise but was captured, as were the other rebel leaders. Two days later, Edward and the Despensers reached Pontefract – that great monument to treachery in their eyes – and the castle immediately surrendered.

After being held at York for four days, Earl Thomas was brought to Pontefract, where Edward and the Younger Despenser 'contemptuously insulted him to his face with malicious and arrogant words', before locking him away in a newly constructed tower in which it was said that he had planned to imprison the king if he ever laid hands on him.[28] The next morning, 22 March, he was brought before a tribunal of seven earls and a royal justice sitting in the great hall where 'he had held many a fair feast', to hear a catalogue of his more notorious crimes and insults to the king over the past decade. The charge, inescapably, was treason, the verdict guilty, the sentence death. When told that (like the Despensers seven months previously) he had no right of reply, he merely remarked that this was 'a powerful court, and very great in authority, where no answer is heard nor any mitigation admitted'. He was immediately led out of the castle to a little hillock outside the walls, the spot from which he and his men had jeered at the king in 1317.[29] Now the jeers were for him. One chronicler likened his last journey to Christ's ascent of Calvary: 'some worthless beast of burden' was found to carry him, and 'upon his head they set an old chaplet, all rent and torn'. There were shouts of 'King Arthur!' and 'Traitor!' Snow lay on the ground, and a few bystanders threw snowballs at him. His last conversation was with a Dominican friar who confessed him. 'Fair father,' he begged, 'stay with me until I am dead, for my flesh quakes for dread of death.' When they reached the summit, Lancaster knelt facing east, but a 'ribald' took hold of him, saying, 'Traitor, look towards the Scots!' 'As you wish,' he replied, and turned to the north, whereupon the friar stepped back and 'this earl, lately the terror of the whole land, stretched forth his neck as if in prayer, and with two or three blows the executioner cut off his head'.[30]

4
'Make it Your Business that We Become Rich'

Edward's triumph in 1321–2 gave him the opportunity to establish strong and responsible rule in England. Despite the return of the Despensers, there was plenty of support for the king – not just the residual loyalty and self-interest of the land- and power-holding elite, but revulsion at the excesses of the Marchers and the stiff-necked obstructionism of Lancaster and his supporters. England ached for peace, and for the first time since his accession Edward could govern on his own terms.

It was an opportunity spectacularly squandered. What followed Earl Thomas's downfall was not sound government but a reign of terror, beginning with the purge of those who had dared to oppose the king and the Despensers. In addition to Lancaster, a further twenty-six barons, knights and esquires were condemned without trial before being drawn, hanged and quartered, the most prominent among them being John de Mowbray, Roger de Clifford, John Giffard and Bartholomew de Badlesmere. To terrorize their adherents, they were executed in their localities – York, Pontefract, Bristol, Gloucester, Windsor, Cambridge, Cardiff, Swansea, Canterbury – and their bodies or what

remained of them left dangling from the gallows or orna-
menting town walls for up to two years.[1] A further one
hundred or so were imprisoned, spared the ultimate penalty
only because, like Maurice de Berkeley or the Mortimers,
they had surrendered just in time. Wives, children and even
parents of Contrariants were also incarcerated, and fines
totalling £17,000 were imposed on their heirs or families.[2]
Those who were executed or imprisoned – at least 117 of
them – also naturally forfeited all their lands and chattels to
the king. The parliament that met at York in May 1322 confirmed these sentences, abolished the Ordinances 'finally
and forever', and outlawed by statute any future attempt to
limit the king's freedom of action.[3] Even Pembroke, upon
whom Edward had relied for so long, was briefly arrested in
June, on the grounds that he had wavered in August 1321 by
advising the king to exile the Despensers in order to save his
throne. 'Terrified by threats and penalties', the nobility 'let
the king's will have free rein'. 'O! The excessive cruelty of
the king and his friends.'[4]

Edward's 'friends' meant primarily the Despensers, who
now entered upon a period of unrivalled dominance. If
Gaveston had been a 'second king', after 1322 there were
'three kings in England'.[5] Hugh the Elder was made Earl of
Winchester and granted lands worth nearly £4,000, while
his son accumulated an estate valued at £7,184 a year and
by 1326 had over £6,000 in cash deposited with Italian
bankers. Two-thirds of his lands were in Wales, where he
effectively reunited the earldom of Gloucester. He was the
richest English landholder apart from the king, who supported his machinations without scruple. Widows were

Despenser's speciality. Roger Damory's widow, Elizabeth – the king's niece, it is worth remembering – was imprisoned and forced by legal chicanery to give up the lordship of Usk. William de Braose's daughter Alina, the widow of John de Mowbray, was threatened with death until her father similarly promised to surrender properties to the Despensers. Lancaster's widow, Alice, was imprisoned at York and told she would be burned alive unless she agreed to hand over the great lordship of Denbigh in north Wales. The widow of Stephen Baret, a Contrariant hanged at Swansea, was tortured until she went out of her mind – it was even alleged that some of her limbs were broken.[6] To resist the Despensers' will was almost impossible: as the author of the *Vita* put it, 'Whatever pleases the king, though lacking in reason, has the force of law'; or, as one petitioner remarked, 'There is no law in the land.'[7]

The Despensers apart, three men were identified as the chief agents of the regime. Edmund, Earl of Arundel was in reality more beneficiary than agent. A year younger than the king, he had joined the opposition during the early part of the reign, but from about 1315, disillusioned with Lancaster, he had become increasingly royalist, a stance cemented by the royally sponsored marriage of his son to the Younger Despenser's daughter in February 1321. A bitter enemy of the Mortimers, he was rewarded in 1322 with their lordship of Chirk, which bordered his lordship of Oswestry (Shropshire). He also received the Mowbray honour of Axholme (Lincolnshire) and acquired considerable movable wealth, although apart from acting as Justice of Wales he had no formal government role after

1322. By contrast, Robert Baldock and Walter Stapeldon were clerics and administrators. Baldock, a protégé of the Younger Despenser, was keeper of the king's privy seal from 1320 to 1323 and chancellor of the realm from 1323 to 1326. Deeply unpopular, he was seen as a willing tool of the regime and fell out badly with several of the bishops, whose promotions he envied. Three times Edward tried to get him elected to a bishopric, and three times he failed. Stapeldon, a man of humble origins but Bishop of Exeter since 1308, was a more equivocal figure: a lawyer, scholar and patron of learning, he was valued by the king for his organizational ability and was the architect of Exchequer reform in the 1320s, but also showed himself willing to stand up to Edward and the Despensers. However, as treasurer of the realm for nearly five years, he was inescapably associated with their scheming, and he certainly acquired much personal wealth.

Behind this cabal loomed the dangerously unpredictable Edward himself, now entering his thirty-ninth year. Chroniclers, including those who supported him, thought that his mind had been 'bewitched' by 'King Hugh', and to some extent this was true, but the evidence of Edward's letters also points to his personal initiative in the regime's rapacity. Burdened by debt from the moment of his accession and obliged thus far to beg, bargain and capitulate in return for funds, Edward had developed 'an obsessive preoccupation with wealth'.[8] Impatient with Exchequer bureaucracy, he directed a stream of sarcastic or menacing orders to his officials to streamline accounting procedures, enforce the levying of fines, debts and arrears, exploit confiscated lands to the full and maximize the yield from the crown's prerogative rights such as *prise*. When they failed to match his expectations, they were harangued or supplanted: hence the appointment in July 1322 of Roger Belers, a Lancastrian renegade who became chief baron of the Exchequer in July 1322 with special responsibility for expropriating the estates of his former master. Although Stapeldon, as treasurer, resented Belers's intrusion, the king's will was done. Ordinances centralizing and reforming Exchequer procedure poured forth during these years. Officials were told to work longer hours, take shorter holidays and in some cases reduced salaries. 'Make it your business that We become rich,' Edward wrote to the treasurer and barons of the Exchequer in September 1323.[9]

And they did. The king's wealth in the later years of the reign became the stuff of legend. He was, said one chronicler, 'the richest king that ever was in England since William [the Conqueror]'; 'many of his predecessors amassed money, but he outstripped them all', claimed the author of the *Vita*.[10] By keeping most of Lancaster's estates for himself, Edward virtually doubled the crown's landed income. The abolition of the Ordinances meant that he was once again free to impose higher customs duties, and in 1322 the heaviest lay subsidy of the reign (£42,000) was granted by Parliament. Receipts for the Exchequer year from April 1323 to April 1324 amounted to a remarkable £114,000. A year and a half later, despite having had to spend around £60,000 on defending Gascony, there was still £69,000 left in the Treasury, which by the autumn of 1326 had swollen to £91,000.[11] Hand in hand with avarice, stringent economies also contributed to the king's ever-growing wealth. In the royal household, expenditure was lower than at any time in the fourteenth century, evidence of the seriousness with which the king took the process of 'becoming rich'.

Yet none of this seemed to guarantee the security Edward craved, least of all in the north, where the expiry of the truce was immediately followed by the renewal of Scottish raiding. January 1322 saw the 'burning of the bishopric', a devastating raid on Durham. Another campaign was needed, and once again Edward planned a massive show of force. Around 20,000 infantry, 2,000 light cavalry and 1,250 heavy cavalry mustered at Newcastle at the beginning of August and some 30 ships loaded with provisions were sent north. Edward's pride in his army – 'such as has never been seen in our time, or in the times of our ancestors'[12] – shows that despite twenty years' experience of campaigning in Scotland he still had not learned from his mistakes. In fact, the army with which his father had won the Battle of Falkirk in 1298 was even larger, around 28,000, but the crucial difference was that Edward I had had both allies and a network of castles and towns in Scotland to serve as supply centres for his troops. By 1322 this was no longer so, and if the fleet failed to make the rendezvous at Edinburgh the English army was doomed, for as usual the Scots had retreated northwards, driving their livestock before them and carrying whatever provisions they could. This was exactly what happened: bad weather, Flemish privateers and Scottish insurgents combined to prevent all but a few of the ships getting through, and three days after reaching Edinburgh on 23 August, with his soldiers starving, Edward called off the campaign and returned to Newcastle.

More effective, as ever, was the Scottish response. Robert Bruce had already raided Cumberland and Lancashire in July, and as soon as the English army turned homewards he sent James Douglas to harry and hurry them on their way. On 30 September, Bruce and Thomas Randolph also crossed the border, and by mid October they were in north Yorkshire. Their aim was to capture Edward, who was staying at Rievaulx Abbey, having dismissed his army. Warned as they were sitting down to breakfast that an attack was imminent, he and the Younger Despenser gathered up what they could and fled to York, reaching the gates of the city just before their pursuers. Isabella, meanwhile, had been left at Tynemouth, where it was believed she would be safe, but having narrowly failed to capture the English king, the Scots now tried to seize the queen instead. Fortunately she managed to escape by sea, but one of her ladies-in-waiting was killed and she must have felt deeply the indignity of once again having to flee. Less fortunate was the Earl of Richmond: captured by Douglas and Randolph near Byland Abbey, he remained a prisoner for nearly two years before being ransomed for £9,333 – the sort of hefty windfall to which Bruce was becoming accustomed. The Scottish king and his captains spent over a month plundering Yorkshire, Northumberland and Cumberland, their most sustained irruption of the reign.

Even with the magnates behind him and no fifth column

in the shape of Thomas of Lancaster to undermine him, the 'ever chicken-hearted and luckless' Edward had managed to notch up yet another crushing humiliation.[13] For Andrew Harclay, who had been made Earl of Carlisle as a reward for his defeat of the Contrariant forces at Boroughbridge, it was the last straw. Despairing of the king's ability to contain the Scottish threat, he arranged secretly to meet Bruce at Lochmaben on 3 January 1323. The terms they agreed were by no means one-sided: Bruce agreed to end Scottish raiding, pay reparations of £26,666 and respect Edward's rule in England. In return, however, he insisted that the English king recognize Scotland as a separate and autonomous kingdom and himself as its rightful king. The 'poor folk, middle class and farmers in the northern parts' were not surprisingly delighted with this, but Scottish independence was something Edward would not concede, and when news of the agreement was leaked to him he pronounced Harclay a traitor and ordered his arrest.[14] The fate of the man who had done more than any other to counter the Scottish threat over the past decade, who had delivered Lancaster a captive to the king, and who ten months earlier had been deemed worthy of an earldom, was thus to be drawn, hanged, decapitated, disembowelled and quartered, his entrails burned before him and his severed head sent south to be suspended from the battlements of the Tower of London.

Yet even Edward and his closest allies were not deluded enough to think that matters could continue as they were, and within another two months Pembroke, the Younger Despenser, Stapeldon and Baldock were sent to negotiate

an end to hostilities. The resulting agreement, ratified at
Bishopsthorpe near York on 30 May 1323, was not a peace
treaty, for Edward refused to deal with 'Robert, King of
Scots', only with 'Sir Robert de Bruce', but both sides
swore to observe a truce for thirteen years, during which
claims on either side of the border would be shelved. For
the first time in a quarter of a century, there was peaceful
coexistence between England and Scotland. Yet, although
the truce of Bishopsthorpe was welcomed by the great
majority, to a few powerful Englishmen whose claims to
lands and titles in Scotland were abandoned it was a
betrayal. Among them was Henry, Lord Beaumont, claim-
ant to the Scottish earldom of Buchan and thus far a
staunch royalist, who protested so vehemently that Edward
briefly imprisoned him. Powerful northern lords such as
Henry Percy of Alnwick and Thomas Wake of Liddell also
felt cheated of their rights. These 'Disinherited' now joined
the ranks of the disaffected.[15]

Those ranks were swelling. If some saw the butchery of
Harclay as evidence of the king's underlying insecurity, to
others it was no more than the upstart Earl of Carlisle
deserved for his role in capturing Lancaster, who in death
was coming to be seen as a symbol of heroic resistance to a
tyrannous regime, a political saint in the tradition of
Simon de Montfort, killed seventy years earlier rebelling
against Henry III and subsequently seen by many as a
martyr to the cause of freedom. Within weeks of Lancaster's 'martyrdom', miraculous cures were being reported at
his grave, 'which are genuine', alleged one contemporary,

'and found to be so by good investigations'.[16] By the summer of 1323, the crowds of dumb, blind and crippled converging on Pontefract were so dense that pilgrims were killed in the crush and the king despatched fourteen of his Gascon henchmen to cordon off the grave.[17] The plaque Lancaster had erected to the Ordinances in St Paul's was also attracting miracle seekers, and in May 1323 Baldock had it removed. Meanwhile, in Bristol, there were reports of both cures and riots at the spot where the weathered corpse of another Contrariant, Sir Henry de Montfort, still swung from the gibbet. Memories were stirred, and when Edward visited Whorlton Castle (Yorkshire) in August 1323, he heard two women singing songs of Simon de Montfort.

Despite the regime's best efforts, a few of the 1321–2 rebels had avoided capture and were now outlaws bent on revenge. Among them was Sir William Trussell, leader of a gang that launched an attack on the Elder Despenser's estates in the Midlands in March 1323.[18] Two months earlier, another group of desperados had only just failed to free Maurice de Berkeley from Wallingford Castle. The unlucky Berkeley died three years later, still in prison, as did Roger Mortimer of Chirk, but not so his nephew, Roger Mortimer of Wigmore. Having held the younger Mortimer in the Tower of London for a year and a half, the king decided in the summer of 1323 that he would after all have him put to death, but on 1 August – the feast, appropriately, of St Peter in Chains – Mortimer escaped by drugging the constable and guards, letting himself down the Tower's riverside wall by a rope ladder, rowing to

Greenwich and fleeing to France. The constable was immediately dismissed by the infuriated king, but what should really have alarmed Edward was the range of Mortimer's accomplices, from the deputy constable, who probably provided the potion and subsequently fled with him after unlocking his cell, to the Londoners – including the former mayor, John de Gisors – who rowed him over the Thames and provided the horses waiting to speed him to the coast, to well-wishers in France, who sheltered him despite Edward's demands that he be returned.[19]

London was by now a hotbed of discontent, not just the city's shifting underclass but also many prominent citizens angered by the high-handed way in which Edward had tried to curtail their civic privileges by instigating an eyre (judicial inquiry) in the city in early 1321. As a result of this, the king had dismissed the mayor and suspended the city's liberties, which were only restored when, under pressure from the Marchers in July 1321, Edward was looking for support wherever he could find it. It was but a brief reconciliation: Londoners were accused of complicity in the attempt to release Maurice de Berkeley as well as in the escape of Mortimer, and in 1323, no longer needing to woo them, Edward again suspended the mayoralty. Later that year, the city gates had to be closed to forestall an attempt to ambush the king.[20] It was with Flemish mercenaries that he now garrisoned the Tower. Walter Stapeldon, seen as the man responsible for the 1321 eyre, was especially hated in the capital, as would soon become clear.

Also suspected of complicity in Mortimer's escape was Adam Orleton, the learned and truculent Bishop of

Hereford. Detested by the king's supporters – the chronicler Geoffrey le Baker described him as having 'a great deal of natural cunning' and a voracious appetite for crime – Orleton was certainly close to Mortimer, whose principal estates lay in Herefordshire, but whether he had actively aided his jailbreak was never established, because the bishop took his stand on clerical privilege and refused to answer in a lay court.[21] When Edward tried to press the point by bringing him before the King's Bench in February 1324, Orleton was saved by the theatrical intervention of the Archbishops of Canterbury, York and Dublin, who, with their processional crosses carried before them, filed into court, took him by the hand and led him away. Edward had the sense not to provoke a clash over the issue of ecclesiastical immunity (which would almost certainly involve the pope), contenting himself with the seizure of Orleton's temporalities, but his relations with the Church were under increasing strain. The Bishops of Lincoln and of Bath and Wells were suspected of sympathy with the Contrariants and in 1323 Edward asked Pope John to remove them from England (which was not done). When the Bishop of Winchester died the same year, Edward tried to secure the see for Baldock, but the pope chose John Stratford. Stratford's rich temporalities were also sequestered and he was summoned to appear before the Younger Despenser. More worrying, however, were the signs that a hitherto supportive papacy was no longer willing to humour the English king. In January 1324, Pope John wrote to say that the continuing interdict on Scotland was imperilling souls there and that he saw no harm in recognizing Robert Bruce as king. In fact, he did not, at least not yet, but he did advise Edward to treat the leading men of his kingdom with greater consideration.[22]

Since the death of Archbishop Winchelsey in 1313, Edward had managed the English Church hierarchy as well as the papacy with a degree of skill. He had also gone out of his way not to antagonize the French, no mean feat during the Franco-Flemish War of 1315–19 when English wool exports were badly disrupted and the king was often obliged to be forceful in protecting English trade and shipping, which he did with considerable success.[23] By 1323, however, relations with France were deteriorating fast. Paris always looked askance at England's tenure of Gascony, and the rapid turnover of French monarchs in the early fourteenth century led to regular demands to perform homage for the duchy, a technically obligatory but demeaning act for an otherwise autonomous ruler. The childless death of Philip V in 1322 brought his brother Charles IV to the throne – the fourth French king in eight years – and he and his influential uncle Charles de Valois, a man with 'a very deep hatred for the English', were a good deal less sympathetic to backsliding than Philip had been.[24] Failing to heed the warning signs, Edward stumbled into war with France, and it proved to be the catalyst for the last and greatest crisis of his reign.

The fuse that would ignite the 'War of Saint-Sardos' was lit on 16 October 1323, when a gang of pro-English Gascons hanged a French royal sergeant from the stake he had just planted in the ground at Saint-Sardos in the Agenais (east-central Gascony) to mark the spot where it was intended to build a bastide (fortified town), a plan to which the English objected. Unfortunately this coincided with a demand from Charles IV that the English king come and do homage for Gascony. Although Edward expressed regret at the outrage, when his officials in Gascony refused to appear in Paris to stand trial, and when he yet again requested that his homage be respited, Charles lost patience and in June 1324 issued a call to arms. Pembroke was sent to mollify the French king, but died on the way. It probably made little difference. The invasion, led by Charles de Valois, began on 14 August, and by the time a truce was agreed seven weeks later, the Agenais had been overrun and with it more than half of Gascony. Blame for this fiasco fell on the Younger Despenser, to whom Edward had effectively committed the conduct of policy in the duchy.[25]

As so often, a quick war was followed by a slow peace. By general agreement, the person most likely to resolve the diplomatic impasse was Queen Isabella, who was also Charles IV's sister, and in March 1325 she crossed the Channel. The negotiations were difficult, but during the summer a draft agreement was reached. Although far from satisfactory from an English point of view, for Charles made it clear that he had no intention of withdrawing, it provided a basis for discussion. First, however, the French wanted Edward to perform homage, and by mid August 1325 he had arrived at Dover, ready to embark. A few days later, however, he changed his mind: instead, he wrote to Charles on 24 August saying he was ill, then returned to London. The French did not believe him, although they could hardly accuse him openly of lying, but many in England too saw it as an unnecessary provocation. In fact, the real reason why Edward would not go to France was probably because the Despensers had asked him not to, on account of the 'imminent danger' to themselves if they were left on their own in England.[26] Fortunately, an alternative was to hand. Instead of the English king in person, his eldest son, already the heir to Gascony, could be invested with the duchy and sent to Paris. And so it was done: Prince Edward, now twelve, crossed the Channel in mid September 1325, accompanied by the Earl of Kent and Walter Stapeldon, and performed homage to Charles IV at Vincennes on 24 September.

With the immediate crisis over homage resolved, the English king expected his wife and son to return to England without further ado, but at this point the worm turned. Before 1322, there was nothing to indicate that Isabella had been anything but a faithful and obedient consort – her fourth child and second daughter, Joan, was born in July 1321 – but after Edward allowed the Younger Despenser to seize some of her lands and dismiss her French servants in September 1324 (on the pretext that they represented a security risk at a time of growing tension with France), she finally lost respect for her husband and grew to loathe his all-powerful favourite. 'I feel,' she declared publicly in Paris, 'that marriage is a union of a man and a woman, holding fast to the practice of a life together, and that someone has come between my husband and myself and is trying to break this bond. I declare that I will not return until this intruder is removed.'[27] Stapeldon fled back to England in fear of his life, but not Prince Edward, whom Isabella kept with her.

Before long, rumours also filtered back to England that the English queen had struck up a liaison with Roger Mortimer. Mortimer was three years younger than Edward and, unlike the king, enjoyed an enviable military reputation, acquired largely in Ireland, where he held great estates and had been active in resisting the Bruces. Edward feared him, and the Despensers detested him, not only for his part in the civil war but also because of a family feud dating back to the Battle of Evesham (1265), where Mortimer's grandfather had been responsible for the death of the Elder Despenser's father.[28] Whether or not it is true that 'the enraged virago [Isabella] had found comfort in [Mortimer's] unlawful embraces' (as Geoffrey le Baker put it), the domineering Mortimer had undoubtedly acquired a strong hold over the queen.[29] Edward may even have considered divorcing her, but the implications for Anglo-French relations were prohibitive.

By the spring of 1326, news of Isabella and Mortimer's liaison and suspicion of their intentions were inducing growing nervousness in England. In February, Edward proclaimed publicly that Isabella was being manipulated by 'the Mortimer' and consorting with him 'both within and outside her household' – thereby mirroring the accusations she was making about him and Despenser.[30] The Earls of Kent and Richmond, the Bishop of Norwich and Henry de Beaumont were also in Paris and said to be in league with the queen. As rumours of impending invasion multiplied, opponents of the regime grew bolder. In January

1326 the reviled chief baron of the exchequer, Roger Belers, was assassinated in Leicestershire. Orders were sent out to move prisoners from jail to jail to foil plans to liberate them; beacons were erected to warn of invasion; coastal defence units were put on standby and castles garrisoned; correspondence to and from the continent was censored. Not since Prince Louis brought a French army to England in 1215 had there been an invasion threat on such a scale. The air of menace that had characterized government since 1322 was becoming more edgy. Letter after letter was despatched to France, reassuring or haranguing the queen, pleading with Prince Edward, trying to bribe French lords, asking Charles IV to send Mortimer and/or Isabella back to England. Yet Charles had no reason to help Edward: tension was on the rise again in Gascony, and in June 1326 there was another outbreak of hostilities in the duchy. A new Franco-Scottish treaty was also agreed in April, raising the possibility of war on two fronts.

On the other hand, the French king could not fail to be aware that Isabella's continued presence at his court while conducting an affair with a public enemy of her husband's kingdom was scandalizing his people, and in July 1326 it was made clear to her that she must move on. Fortunately for her, she had a trump to play: the hand in marriage of the future King of England. She had already been in touch with several rulers in the Low Countries, and now concluded a deal: on 27 August, less than a month after leaving France, Prince Edward was betrothed to Philippa, daughter of Count William of Hainault, in return for which the count provided 700 mercenaries under the command of his brother John. The retinues of English exiles – principally the Earls of Kent and Richmond, Henry de Beaumont, William Trussell and Mortimer himself – added roughly the same number again. Financed by Philippa of Hainault's dowry, the force with which Isabella invaded her husband's kingdom sailed from Dordrecht in Holland on 22 September and disembarked two days later at Orwell (Suffolk).

News of his wife's landing was brought to Edward in the Tower of London on 27 September. The Elder Despenser seems to have realized at once that the game was up: she would never have dared to land with such a small force, he declared, if she had not known that the country would rise with her.[31] Attempts were made to rally the Londoners, but the city was in an ugly mood. When Archbishop Reynolds read out in St Paul's Cathedral on 30 September a bull of excommunication against the invaders, he failed to disclose its date; his audience, who knew that it had been issued six years earlier against the Scots, simply jeered.[32] Two days later, with the royal administration decimated by desertions, the king, Baldock and the Despensers fled towards Wales, hoping to enlist the forces that had helped defeat the Marchers in 1322. Barely had they left when the city erupted. John the Marshal, a Despenser spy, was dragged from his house and beheaded in Cheapside. Stapeldon was warned of the danger as he approached the city; scurrying to St Paul's for sanctuary, he was seized at the north door, wrenched from his horse, hauled through the cemetery to Cheapside and there decapitated with a bread knife along with two of his servants. His body was cast on a rubbish tip and his head sent to Queen Isabella. He was the first English bishop to be murdered since Thomas Becket in 1170. His death sparked an orgy of looting, with thousands of pounds in cash and jewels rifled from the deposits which the Younger Despenser, the Earl of Arundel, Baldock, Stapeldon and others held in the city's churches and banking houses (the looters were known as the 'Rifflers').[33] The Tower was emptied of prisoners and Lancaster's memorial to the Ordinances re-erected in St Paul's.

By the time Stapeldon's head was brought to her, Isabella's army had reached Gloucester. From the day she landed, supporters had flocked to her – earls, bishops, barons, outlaws and many besides. Wisely, she put it about that it was the Younger Despenser and other 'traitors' she had come to destroy, not 'our beloved lord the king'. Whether or not she was believed, England barely lifted a finger to stop her. On 22 October she reached Bristol, which surrendered almost at once: the Elder Despenser, to whom Edward had entrusted its custody, was tried for treason on 27 October. No mercy could be expected, and none was allowed. Having denied any right of reply to Lancaster, he was told that he would be judged according to his own law: drawn by horses to the public gallows, he was hanged, cut down while still alive and beheaded. His head was sent to Winchester, the seat of his earldom, and his arms destroyed for ever, since he had dishonoured the name of chivalry. 'How sad it is,' remarked one chronicler, 'that such a man, pre-eminent in his own times for his sense and probity, should act so foolishly at the end of his life.'[34]

Meanwhile, on 20 October, Edward, the Younger

Despenser and Baldock had sailed from Chepstow in the hope of reaching Ireland. Had they done so, they might have been able to flee to the continent or even launch a counter-invasion of England, but storms blew them back to Cardiff, whence they made their way to Despenser's great castle at Caerphilly. They had brought £29,000 of silver coin in barrels to pay men to fight for them, but no one was foolish enough to accept it. Even so, Caerphilly was one of the most defensible fortresses in Britain – remarkably, it was not surrendered until April 1327 – and had the king decided to stay there it is not out of the question that terms of some sort might yet have been negotiated. Instead, for reasons unknown, he fled west, accompanied by Despenser and Baldock. Between 2 and 10 November they were at Neath Abbey, where Edward's last known act as a free man was to appoint the abbot and others to go and speak with 'our most beloved consort' Isabella and their son, but it was too late for that.[35] The next day, having failed to find a refuge, a passage abroad, or a miracle, they retraced their steps eastwards. Hunted by now throughout south Wales, they were cornered near Llantrisant Castle on 16 November, a day of fearsome storms, by a party led by Thomas of Lancaster's brother Henry, now Earl of Leicester. The spot where the king was captured is known as Pant-y-brad, the Vale of Treachery.

From Llantrisant, Edward was taken to Monmouth, where he was obliged to surrender the great seal of England, thereby ending his rule (though not yet his reign). Baldock was handed to Bishop Orleton and sent to London; he died six months later in the Fleet prison, 'a dog among thieves'.[36]

The Younger Despenser was taken to Hereford, where, on the day following the king's capture, the Earl of Arundel had been beheaded – by 'the vilest of ruffians', it was said, who took twenty-two blows to sever his head.[37] Under no illusion about what awaited him, Despenser tried to starve himself by refusing food and water. Isabella and Mortimer probably hoped to take him to London, but he was too weak and had to be executed at Hereford. Convicted of treason, usurping royal power and a multitude of other crimes, he was spared no embellishment. A ladder fifty feet high was erected so all could witness his torments: bound in chains and drawn there on a hurdle on 24 November, confessing his sins, 'his eyes bulging with terror', he was hanged until almost dead, then castrated and disembowelled before being brought down and decapitated. His body was quartered and distributed around the country, his head impaled on London Bridge. The chroniclers exulted: 'By God's ordaining, the project of Achitophel was confounded'; 'And so died the traitors of England, and blessed be Almighty God!'[38]

A week later, Edward was moved to the Lancastrian stronghold of Kenilworth in Warwickshire to await his fate. Shortly before Christmas, at a council held at Wallingford, the decision was taken not to put him to death; that he would be deposed was, however, widely accepted by now. The problem was how, for no English king had been deposed before, and to depose an anointed monarch was against God and the law. The solution, arrived at in a quasi-parliamentary assembly summoned to Westminster for 7 January 1327, was not to depose him but to oblige him to abdicate, to which end two delegations were sent to Kenilworth. To the first, around 10 January, Edward apparently expressed regret for his misdeeds but no more. When this was reported to the assembly on 12 January, the magnates and prelates were asked whether they wished him to continue ruling over them. Egged on by a baying London mob, they cried out for his removal; if there was opposition, it was airbrushed from the record. A memorandum was drawn up listing the reasons why 'Edward, the eldest son of the king, should have the government of the realm and be crowned as king'. Edward II was charged with having always been badly led by others and thus being inadequate; of failing to apply himself to the business of ruling, instead giving himself up to 'inappropriate occupations'; of losing Scotland and territories in Ireland and Gascony, which his father was said, disingenuously, to have left to him at peace; of persecuting prelates and magnates; of failing to do justice to his people or keep his coronation oath; of abandoning his kingdom; and, by his cruelty and misdeeds, of showing himself to be beyond hope of reform; all of which was said to be so well known that no one could deny it.[39]

The second delegation to Kenilworth, comprising twenty-four representatives of all the estates of the realm, was led by Bishops Orleton and Stratford and Henry, Earl of Leicester. Isabella, her children, Mortimer, and the king's half-brothers, Kent and Norfolk (both of whom had supported the revolution), remained in London – indeed Edward never saw his wife or children again, Isabella claiming implausibly that she could not visit him for fear of what he might do to her. Arriving at Kenilworth on 20 January, the delegates told the king what had been agreed at Westminster. According to the eyewitness account preserved in Geoffrey le Baker's chronicle, he was wearing a black gown, and was so distraught when he first emerged from his chamber that 'in the shock of sorrow he lost his wits and collapsed in a heap on the floor'. Raised to his feet by Stratford and Leicester, he was asked to resign his crown. It was, he was told, a way for him to make his peace with God and his people; he would continue to be treated with honour, and his eldest son would succeed him. If, however, he refused to abdicate, then someone 'not of the royal blood' might be chosen as king instead – a threat hard to credit, for it would assuredly have brought civil war. 'With tears and lamentations', Edward eventually agreed. The formal renunciation of homage to 'Sir Edward of Caernarvon' was performed the next day by Sir William Trussell on behalf of all the estates, whereupon the delegates returned to Westminster to announce that the king had, 'of his good will, removed himself from the government of the kingdom'.[40] Edward was forty-two, and his reign was over. That of Edward III began on 25 January 1327, and on 2 February the new king, now fourteen, was crowned.

For the next two months, the former king remained at Kenilworth, but in early April, following an attempt to free him, he was moved to Berkeley Castle. Claims were later made that he was taunted and abused by his jailers, but the £5 a day allocated for his maintenance implies a reasonable standard of comfort.[41] However, plots to release him continued to be hatched, mostly by Dominican friars (and on one occasion he was briefly liberated from his cell, though not from the castle), so in July he was moved secretly to Corfe Castle (Dorset), and perhaps also to Bristol, before being returned to Berkeley. It was probably information about yet another conspiracy received by Roger Mortimer in mid September 1327 that sealed Edward's fate. The date of his murder was 21 September. The suspected perpetrators – Thomas Gurney, William Ockley and John Maltravers – were all servants of Mortimer's, and in 1330 Edward III publicly accused Mortimer of being the author of the deed. Yet although it took three years for the accusation to be made public, it is hard to think that there were many who believed the official line that the former king had died a natural death. Exactly how Edward died, however, will always be a mystery. The most lurid account – that he was killed by having a red-hot 'iron', or poker, inserted through a tube into his anus – only emerged several years later. It is more likely, as reported by a number of chroniclers, that he was suffocated. Even Geoffrey le Baker, who disseminated the 'poker' story, stated that, before it was inserted, the king was 'smothered and suffocated with great, heavy mattresses'.[42]

Custom and pressure of business meant that three months passed until Edward was buried. In the meantime, his body was embalmed and his heart removed, encased in a silver vase and given to Queen Isabella, who kept it until her own death in 1358, when she was buried in the gown in which she had been married fifty years earlier and Edward's heart was placed in a cavity in the breast of her tomb effigy.[43] Was this a belated act of expiation, a reaffirmation of the mingled French and English blood that fuelled Edward III's bid for the French crown, or even some lingering affection for her dead husband? If the latter, it had not extended to burying him in Westminster Abbey, which was presumably seen as inappropriate or even injudicious for a deposed monarch. In other respects, however, Edward's funeral in Gloucester Abbey (now Cathedral) on 20 December 1327 was a regal and well-attended affair, and accounts of the expenditure incurred there referred to him unhesitatingly as king. A line was being drawn, the mess cleared away. The delicate, spiky canopy which rises exquisitely above his alabaster effigy and Purbeck marble tomb chest is but one of the glories of Gloucester's remodelled perpendicular choir, much of which was paid for by offerings at his tomb.

5
Imagining Edward

The lonely deaths of dethroned kings rarely passed uncontested in the Middle Ages. In March 1330, the Earl of Kent was beheaded for treason after claiming to have been asked by the pope to free Edward II from Corfe Castle, where, so he had been informed, the former king, far from being dead and buried, was still being held. The Archbishop of York also seems by 1330 to have come to believe the story, but not Pope John, who declared that he knew full well that Edward was dead, and eight months later, when it was Roger Mortimer's turn to be executed for treason – having lorded it over king, queen and country for four years and become as hated as the king he had deposed – one of the charges against him was that he had set out to entrap Kent.[1] Yet rumours of Edward's survival persisted. In 1338, an impostor called William le Galeys was brought before Edward III at Koblenz, claiming to be his father. This was probably the same 'Edward II' whom a papal notary, Manuel de Fieschi, had encountered in Italy a year or two earlier, living as a hermit after allegedly escaping from Berkeley Castle and wandering around Britain and the continent for several years. Little is known about le Galeys, who was presumably deluded. Although pressed at times with vigour, the case for Edward II's survival after September 1327 never commanded much support.[2]

Nor did the case for his canonization. England had a tradition of 'political saints' such as Thomas Becket and Simon de Montfort, whose violent deaths in the cause of opposition to 'tyranny' encouraged belief in their sanctity. The fact that Thomas of Lancaster was now being memorialized within this tradition (the parliament of 1327 recommended that the pope be asked to canonize both Lancaster and Robert Winchelsey, the two foremost champions of the Ordinances)[3] made it doubly important for Edward II's sympathizers to follow suit. Edward III neither strongly encouraged nor discouraged his father's cult – there was, after all, nothing to be lost by being the son of a saint – and it acquired a minority following. Richard II (1377–99), on the other hand, who regarded the deposition of his great-grandfather as the great stigma on the history of the English monarchy, took up his cause with enthusiasm, ordering the compilation of a book of Edward's 'miracles' and sending high-ranking prelates to Rome to lobby on his behalf. When Richard in turn was deposed in 1399, however, the momentum was lost. It was Lancaster's cult, always more popular, which survived through the fifteenth century, only to be superseded following the deposition and murder of yet another royal 'martyr', Henry VI, in 1471. As Ranulf Higden pointed out around 1350, Edward II's vices were too notorious for his cult to be credible: incarceration, a horrible death, even rumours of miracles could not compensate for a vicious life; it was 'women who love to wander around', said the monk of Chester, who spread stories of his veneration, but it was 'a house built on sand'.[4]

If in death Edward's vices undermined the case for his sainthood, in life they were used to undermine the moral authority of his kingship. Whether or not his relations with Gaveston and/or the Younger Despenser were sexual is unknowable, but the accusation – first publicly made, as far as is known, by Bishop Orleton in sermons delivered in October and December 1326, when he labelled the king 'a tyrant and a sodomite' – melded easily with the stories already circulating about his 'unseemly' behaviour. Popular ridicule at the king's rowing and digging arose not only because the fourteenth-century paradigm of kingship could not accommodate a 'Farmer George' prototype. Edward's 'eccentricities' were also seen as degenerate – that is to say, indicative of an aberrant and arguably depraved character. Similar arguments were made about heretics (the trial of the Templars in 1311–12 included accusations of both heresy and sodomy), and it is worth noting that the chronicler Jean le Bel stated that the reason why the Younger Despenser was castrated in 1326 was because 'he was a heretic and a sodomite, even, it was said, with the king'. He did not mean that Hugh held heterodox religious opinions, but that, like heretics, his behaviour was contrary to human nature. During the winter of 1325–6, Edward tried to counter such criticism by pointing the finger at his wife, who had fallen under Mortimer's spell and 'succumbed to the wilful pleasure of woman'. Isabella's retort that someone had 'come between' her and her husband, along with Orleton's sermons and the charge in January 1327 that the king was 'incorrigible and without hope of amendment', were an attempt to recapture the moral high ground. It may also have been in this context that the 'poker' version of Edward's death emerged in the mid 1330s, with its connotation that he was not just degenerate but a catamite, 'not the sodomiser but the sodomised'.[5]

What was disturbing was the dichotomy between Edward's behaviour and his almost Olympian view of kingly office. The latter he learned from his father, but whereas Edward I acknowledged (albeit reluctantly) that there were in the end limits to kingly power, his son seems to have been unable to conceive of opposition to his will as anything other than disloyalty. Edward II was enormously stubborn. He was also devious and untrustworthy, continually making promises he had no intention of keeping. He evidently saw nothing wrong in such behaviour: it was his birthright, his prerogative. Paradoxically, on the two occasions when he had the opportunity to exercise the unencumbered power he cherished – at his accession in 1307 and after his triumph in 1322 – he promptly surrendered much of it to favourites. Yet, if at times Edward appeared submissive or simply indolent, he was nevertheless capable of bursts of energy in the pursuit of his goals: to 'become rich', for example, or to destroy the 'traitor' Robert Bruce. It was not lack of desire that prevented Edward from regaining Scotland, but tactical inflexibility, internal dissension and a formidable opponent. What was needed was application and adaptability – qualities Edward lacked. The energy he displayed was not so much mental as temperamental, manifested in destructive explosions of rage, the most spectacular of which saw Andrew Harclay, the one man who showed himself capable of implementing an effective tactical response to the Scots, end his life on the gallows less than a year after being promoted to an earldom.

The grimly inventive repertoire of punishments meted out by both sides during Edward's reign proclaims it as an age of visceral hatreds and almost unparalleled savagery within the English ruling class. Before 1312, no English earl had been executed since 1076; after 1330, it would be nearly sixty years until another was condemned for treason. If it was the murder of Gaveston that set the tone, those responsible for his death could with justification claim that every other option had been tried, and the king's revenge in 1322 was wholly disproportionate. Not that Lancaster showed any more mercy or imagination than the king – indeed, with one or two exceptions such as Pembroke, none of the chief protagonists of the reign emerges with much credit. Ultimately, however, it was Edward's inability to fulfil the two overriding obligations of a medieval king – to administer the law without partiality, and to defend his realm – that lay at the heart of his tragedy. This was a very personal failure, the collapse of the moral authority of Edward's kingship, a resounding endorsement of Aristotle's much-quoted dictum that a ruler who could not control his private passions would not be able to control his kingdom.

Just how personal is indicated by what followed. The first deposition of a reigning English monarch did not lead to any questioning of the institution or attributes of monarchy. Indeed it is remarkable, once Edward III had rid himself of Mortimer, how rapidly he managed not just to reassert royal authority in England but also to restore

English control of southern Scotland and to move on to the offensive against France, a strategy triumphantly vindicated in the 1360 Treaty of Brétigny, when he secured a vastly enlarged Gascony comprising around a quarter of the French kingdom in full sovereignty. With hindsight, to be sure, Edward II's reign can be seen to have marked a turning point in the fortunes of England's 'empire': it would be hard to think of an English king who did more than him to ensure that, until the union of the crowns in 1603, Scotland would remain an independent kingdom. Robert Bruce's achievement was to rescue Scottish kingship from the oblivion into which Edward I had sought to cast it and to reassert the identity of a culturally distinct nation in danger of being smothered by its overmighty neighbour. Meanwhile, the Bruce invasion of Ireland, even if it ended in personal disaster, showed that it was not just in Scotland that the seemingly inexorable advance of English domination of the British Isles could be challenged or even reversed. Yet to have predicted such outcomes in the 1340s or 1350s would have taken uncommon prescience.

Nevertheless, the detritus of Edward's reign did not simply blow away. The grudges, claims and counter-claims spawned by the bitter feuds of the 1320s, although kept in check for fifty years by the consensual politics practised by Edward III, were not forgotten and came back to cull another generation of English nobles at the end of the fourteenth century. Like Edward II, Richard II fell under the sway of favourites and coveted land and wealth for both them and himself. Once again the power of the crown was used to overmaster the law, and once again lords of

Lancaster, Arundel, Warwick, Kent, Despenser, Mortimer, Mowbray and Montague, the grandchildren and great-grandchildren of Edward II's friends and foes, were set at odds with each other, old claims resurrected, executions and forfeitures for treason decreed. It was not simply to rehabilitate his great-grandfather's reputation that Richard sought his canonization. His real aim was to reunite the Lancastrian inheritance with the crown, as Edward had briefly done.[6] The irony is that this is exactly what came to pass, for it was Richard's confiscation of the duchy of Lancaster in March 1399 that led directly to his deposition six months later, and it was the Duke of Lancaster, Henry of Bolingbroke, who replaced him. It was Henry IV who wrote the final chapter of the tragedy of Edward II.

Never again was Edward's cause championed with the passion displayed by Richard. Lancastrian kings had no interest in defending him, let alone sanctifying him, and although in the late sixteenth century the historian Raphael Holinshed tried to present a balanced portrait of the king, the titles of works by poets and dramatists of the time bear ample testimony to his popular reputation: *The History of the Most Unfortunate Prince King Edward II* (Elizabeth Cary, 1627); *The Deplorable Life and Death of Edward II* (Francis Hubert, 1628). The 1590s witnessed a surge of interest in Edward, inspired by French politics of the time: in 1588, Jean Boucher had written the *Histoire tragique et mémorable de Pierre de Gaverston, gentilhomme gascon, jadis mignon d'Edouarde II*, a satire against the duc d'Epernon, another Gascon and one of the notorious *mignons* of the French King Henry III. During the 1590s, the English poet and playwright Michael Drayton devoted four lengthy historical poems to the reign, including *The Mirror for Magistrates: Peirs Gaveston* (1593) and *The Lamentable Civil Wars of Edward the Second and the Barons* (1596).

Much better remembered is Christopher Marlowe's play of 1593, *The Troublesome Raigne and Lamentable Death of Edward the Second, with the Tragicall Fall of Proude Mortimer*, a title further extended in the 1598 edition to include *And also the Life and Death of Peirs Gaveston, the Great Earle of Cornewall and Mighty Favorite of King Edward*. Both Drayton and Marlowe were probably homosexual, and the focus in the 1590s on Edward's unambiguously sexual relationship with his 'minions' and on the king's parodic murder with a 'red-hot spit' decisively influenced later representations of the reign such as the Pre-Raphaelite Marcus Stone's painting of Edward and Gaveston, exhibited at the Royal Academy in 1872.[7] His deposition apart, the two most commonly repeated 'facts' about him today are that he was homosexual and that he was murdered by being impaled with a poker; in 1908, the British Board of Education coyly recommended to schools that his reign 'be passed over in discreet silence'.[8]

Following the 'outing' of gay culture in the 1970s and 1980s, however, Edward and Gaveston were reclaimed as gay icons, most memorably in Derek Jarman's flamboyantly homoerotic film *Edward II* (1991), where the court is a theatre of licentiousness and crowd scenes metamorphose into Gay Rights marches. The next year saw the publication by the Gay Men's Press of Chris Hunt's similarly explicit novel *Gaveston*, in which the king celebrates and laments the love of his favourite and even the breach between Edward and Lancaster is depicted as springing from sexual jealousy. Less attuned to the late twentieth century was Mel Gibson's homage to William Wallace, *Braveheart* (1995), which shows Edward as a foppish ninny who did not even father his heir. At the end of the film, as Wallace is eviscerated before being decapitated, he cries out 'Freedom', neatly foreshadowing the great scream of Edward II that 'will raise the town' as he in turn is skewered twenty years later.[9]

Yet it would be misleading to allow sexual politics to hijack the enduring moral of the reign. It was not the nature of Edward's relationships with Gaveston and the Younger Despenser that lay at the root of his failure, but their intensity and exclusivity. A king who was prepared to 'set aside his kingdom for a minion' would sooner or later forfeit the respect of his nobles, and that was ultimately what brought about his downfall.[10] Explaining why he was the first English king to be deposed is in many ways easier than explaining why it took twenty traumatic years to happen. Edward faced challenges that would have tested the abilities of any king; his singular quality was the talent he possessed for alienating those who could have helped him to overcome them.

Notes

Unless drawn from an edition that includes an English translation, quotations from Latin, Old French or Middle English sources have been translated by the author.

ABBREVIATIONS

Anonimalle	*Anonimalle Chronicle 1307 to 1334*, ed. and trans. W. Childs and J. Taylor (Leeds: Yorkshire Archaeological Society, 1991)
Brut	*The Brut or Chronicles of England*, ed. F. Brie, 2 vols (London: Early English Text Society, 1906–8), I
Chaplais	P. Chaplais, *Piers Gaveston: Edward II's Adoptive Brother* (Oxford: Clarendon Press, 1994)
Dodd and Musson	*The Reign of Edward II: New Perspectives*, ed. G. Dodd and A. Musson (Woodbridge: York Medieval Press, 2006)
Fryde	N. Fryde, *The Tyranny and Fall of Edward II, 1321–1326* (Cambridge: Cambridge University Press, 1979)
Geoffrey le Baker	*The Chronicle of Geoffrey le Baker of Swinbrook*, ed. and trans. D. Preest and R. Barber (Woodbridge: Boydell Press, 2012)
Haines	R. M. Haines, *King Edward II: Edward of Caernarfon, His Life, His Reign, and Its Aftermath* (Montreal and London: McGill-Queen's University Press, 2003)
Johnstone	H. Johnstone, *Edward of Carnarvon, 1284–1307* (Manchester: Manchester University Press, 1946)
Lanercost	*The Chronicle of Lanercost, 1272–1346*, ed. and trans. H. Maxwell (Glasgow: Glasgow University Press, 1913)
Maddicott	J. R. Maddicott, *Thomas of Lancaster, 1307–1322: A Study in the Reign of Edward II* (Oxford: Oxford University Press, 1970)
Phillips	J. R. S. Phillips, *Edward II* (New Haven, Conn., and London: Yale University Press, 2010)
Scalacronica	Sir Thomas Gray, *Scalacronica 1272–1363*, ed. and trans A. King, Publications of the Surtees Society, vol. 209 (Woodbridge: Boydell Press, 2005)
Select Documents	*Select Documents of English Constitutional History 1307–1485*, ed. S. Chrimes and A. Brown (London: Adam & Charles Black, 1961)
Stubbs	*Chronicles of the Reigns of Edward I and Edward II*, ed. W. Stubbs, Rolls Series, 2 vols (London: 1882–3)
Vita	*Vita Edwardi Secundi: The Life of Edward the Second*, ed. and trans. W. Childs, Oxford Medieval Texts (Oxford: Clarendon Press, 2005)

PREFACE

1. *Vita*, p. 200; Phillips, p. 38.

1. 'MY BROTHER PIERS'

1. *Polychronicon Ranulphi Higden*, ed. J. R. Lumby, Rolls Series, 9 vols (London: 1882), VIII, pp. 297–9.
2. J. R. S. Phillips, 'The Reputation of a King: Edward II from Chronicle and Written Record to Compact Disc and Internet', in *European Encounters: Essays in Memory of Albert Lovett*, ed. J. Devlin and H. Clarke (Dublin: University College Dublin Press, 2003), pp. 37–54; Phillips, pp. 5–32; *Vita*, p. 69; quotes in Johnstone, pp. 130–31.
3. Quoted in M. Prestwich, 'The Court of Edward II', in Dodd and Musson, pp. 61–75; Haines, p. 359.
4. 'Annales Bridlingtoniensis', in Stubbs, II, p. 97.
5. Quoted in Johnstone, pp. 13, 64.
6. Fryde, pp. 127, 159; Dodd and Musson, p. 2 (Introduction); Phillips, p. 32.
7. Prestwich, 'The Court of Edward II', in Dodd and Musson, pp. 74–5; Phillips, pp. 61–3.
8. M. Prestwich, *Edward I* (Berkeley, Calif.: University of California Press, 1988), pp. 469–516.
9. Quoted in Johnstone, pp. 97–8.
10. Quoted in Johnstone, pp. 100–101.
11. Quoted in Johnstone, pp. 123–4.
12. Quoted in Chaplais, pp. 7–8.
13. Quoted in Chaplais, pp. 11–13.
14. *Lanercost*, p. 18; Chaplais, pp. 6–22; *Vita*, pp. 28–9.
15. Chaplais, pp. 101–3.
16. J. Hamilton, *Piers Gaveston: Earl of Cornwall, 1307–1312: Politics and Patronage in the Reign of Edward II* (Detroit and London: Wayne State University Press, 1988), p. 44; 'Annales Paulini', in Stubbs, I, p. 259.
17. *Vita*, p. 8.
18. Hamilton, *Piers Gaveston*, p. 47.
19. *Select Documents*, p. 4.
20. Phillips, pp. 145–6.
21. *Vita*, p. 9.
22. *Vita*, p. 11.
23. *Select Documents*, pp. 4–6.
24. *Vita*, pp. 16–17.
25. *Vita*, p. 19.
26. *Select Documents*, pp. 11–17.
27. *Select Documents*, pp. 11–19 (Gaveston: clause 20).
28. *Vita*, p. 33.
29. *Select Documents*, pp. 11–19 (Gaveston: clause 20).
30. *Vita*, pp. 44–9.

2. KING HOBBE AND COUSIN THOMAS

1. *Vita*, pp. 68–70.
2. *Vita*, p. 75.
3. *Vita*, pp. 88–93; M. Brown, *Bannockburn: The Scottish War and the British Isles, 1307–1323* (Edinburgh: Edinburgh University Press, 2008), pp. 115–36.
4. *Scalacronica*, p. 75.
5. *Scalacronica*, pp. 74–7.
6. *Johannis de Trokelowe et Henrici Blaneforde, Chronica et Annales*, ed. H. T. Riley, Rolls Series (London: 1866), p. 86; *Lanercost*, pp. 208–9; *Scalacronica*, p. 77.
7. *Lanercost*, p. 215; *Vita*, p. 96.
8. Brown, *Bannockburn*, p. 6.
9. C. McNamee, *The Wars of the Bruces: Scotland, England and Ireland, 1306–1328* (East Linton: Tuckwell Press, 1997), pp. 72–122.
10. *Vita*, p. 50.
11. Quoted in Maddicott, p. 6.
12. Maddicott, p. 318.
13. Ibid.; *Vita*, p. 57.
14. Maddicott, pp. 107–8.
15. Quoted in J. R. Maddicott, 'Thomas of Lancaster', *Oxford Dictionary of National Biography* (online edition).
16. J. R. Maddicott, *The English Peasantry and the Demands of the Crown, 1294–1341*, *Past and Present* Supplement No. 1 (Oxford: Past and Present Society, 1975).
17. Fryde, pp. 22, 166.
18. *Vita*, p. 108.
19. W. C. Jordan, *The Great Famine: Northern Europe in the Early Fourteenth Century* (Princeton, NJ: Princeton University Press, 1996).
20. *Anonimalle*, p. 90.
21. Despite dating from the early fourteenth century, the Queen Mary Psalter is named after Mary Tudor, to whom it was presented in the mid sixteenth century: K. Smith, 'History, Typology and Homily: The Joseph Cycle in the Queen Mary Psalter', *Gesta* 32 (1993), pp. 147–59; A. R. Stanton, *The Queen Mary Psalter: A Study of Affect and Audience* (Philadelphia: American Philosophical Society, 2001), pp. 106–8.
22. J. Evans, *The Oxford History of English Art 1307–1461* (Oxford: Clarendon Press, 1949), pp. 23, 177.
23. Quoted in McNamee, *The Wars of the Bruces*, p. 153.
24. *Parliament Rolls of Medieval England 1275–1504*, 16 vols (Woodbridge: Boydell Press, 2005), III: *Edward II, 1307–1327*, ed. Seymour Phillips, pp. 205–6.
25. *Lanercost*, p. 217.
26. *Flores Historiarum*, ed. H. R. Luard, Rolls Series, 3 vols (London: 1890), III, p. 178.
27. Maddicott, p. 191; Phillips, p. 294.
28. Quoted in Maddicott, p. 197.
29. J. R. S. Phillips, *Aymer de Valence, Earl of Pembroke 1307–1324: Baronial Politics in the Reign of Edward II* (Oxford: Oxford University Press, 1972), Appendix 3, pp. 312–15.

30. Phillips, pp. 286–7; *Vita*, p. 136.
31. Maddicott, pp. 207–8.
32. *Vita*, p. 130.
33. *Lanercost*, p. 220; *Scalacronica*, p. 79.
34. Quoted in Haines, p. 113.
35. *Vita*, p. 156.

3. 'THE KING'S RIGHT EYE'

1. Quoted in W. Childs, 'Welcome, my Brother: Edward II, John of Powderham and the Chronicles, 1318', in *Church and Chronicle in the Middle Ages: Essays Presented to John Taylor*, ed. I. Wood and G. Loud (London: Hambledon Press, 1991), pp. 149–63.
2. *Lanercost*, pp. 221–4; *Anonimalle*, p. 95; *Vita*, pp. 149, 153.
3. Quoted in Maddicott, p. 247.
4. *Vita*, p. 167.
5. M. Lawrence, 'Rise of a Royal Favourite: The Early Career of Hugh Despenser the Elder', in Dodd and Musson, pp. 205–19.
6. *Anonimalle*, p. 92; *Scalacronica*, p. 89; *Geoffrey le Baker*, pp. 6, 10.
7. *Lanercost*, p. 229.
8. Prestwich, 'The Court of Edward II', in Dodd and Musson, p. 71.
9. *Calendar of Ancient Correspondence Concerning Wales*, ed. J. G. Edwards (Cardiff: University of Wales Press, 1935), pp. 219–20.
10. *Vita*, p. 183.
11. B. Wells-Furby, 'The Gower Prelude to the Marcher Rising of 1321: A Question of Evidence', *Welsh History Review* 27 (2014), pp. 4–27.
12. Quoted in Phillips, pp. 358–9; Maddicott, p. 257.
13. *Vita*, pp. 184, 188.
14. B. Wells-Furby, 'The Contrariant Uprising of 1321–2: A New Perspective', *Transactions of the Bristol and Gloucestershire Archaeological Association* 130 (2012), pp. 183–97; A. Tebbit, 'Household Knights and Military Service Under the Direction of Edward II', in Dodd and Musson, pp. 76–96; M. Prestwich, 'The Unreliability of Royal Household Knights in the Early Fourteenth Century', in *Fourteenth Century England*, vol. 2, ed. C. Given-Wilson (Woodbridge: Boydell Press, 2002), pp. 1–11.
15. *Geoffrey le Baker*, p. 10.
16. *Vita*, p. 189.
17. *Vita*, p. 191.
18. *Brut*, p. 213.
19. *Parliamentary Texts of the Later Middle Ages*, ed. N. Pronay and J. Taylor (Oxford: Oxford University Press, 1980), p. 162.
20. *Parliamentary Texts*, ed. Pronay and Taylor, pp. 157–64.
21. Ibid.
22. *Vita*, p. 197.
23. *Vita*, p. 199.
24. J. Beverley Smith, 'Edward II and the Allegiance of Wales', *Welsh History Review* 8 (1976–7), pp. 139–71.

25. *Brut*, p. 216.
26. K. de Vries, *Infantry Warfare in the Early Fourteenth Century* (Woodbridge: Boydell Press, 1996), pp. 86–99; *Lanercost*, p. 231.
27. *Geoffrey le Baker*, p. 13.
28. *Anonimalle*, p. 107; *Vita*, p. 213.
29. *Vita*, p. 215; *Scalacronica*, p. 87; *Brut*, p. 222.
30. *Brut*, pp. 222–3; *Vita*, p. 215.

4. 'MAKE IT YOUR BUSINESS THAT WE BECOME RICH'

1. Fryde, pp. 61–2; *Brut*, p. 224.
2. M. Buck, *Politics, Finance and the Church in the Reign of Edward II: Walter Stapeldon, Treasurer of England* (Cambridge: Cambridge University Press, 1983), p. 174.
3. *English Historical Documents, III: 1189–1327*, ed. H. Rothwell (London: Eyre and Spottiswoode, 1975), pp. 543–4.
4. *Lanercost*, p. 235; *Vita*, p. 231.
5. *Geoffrey le Baker*, p. 16.
6. Fryde, pp. 112–17; Phillips, pp. 446–8.
7. *Vita*, p. 231; The National Archives, Kew, SC 8/143/7102 (Ancient Petition, 1325).
8. Fryde, p. 87.
9. Quoted in Fryde, pp. 87, 94, 98; Haines, p. 38.
10. *Brut*, p. 225; *Vita*, p. 231.
11. Fryde, p. 105; Buck, *Politics, Finance and the Church*, p. 193.
12. Quoted in Phillips, p. 430.
13. *Lanercost*, p. 240.
14. *Lanercost*, p. 242.
15. R. Nicholson, *Edward III and the Scots: The Formative Years of a Military Career, 1327–1335* (Oxford: Oxford University Press, 1965).
16. *Anonimalle*, p. 113.
17. *Brut*, pp. 228–30; Fryde, p. 153.
18. Fryde, pp. 150–52.
19. I. Mortimer, *The Greatest Traitor: The Life of Sir Roger Mortimer, 1st Earl of March, Ruler of England, 1327–1330* (London: Jonathan Cape, 2003), pp. 130–34; Phillips, p. 460.
20. Haines, p. 168.
21. *Geoffrey le Baker*, pp. 15–16.
22. Phillips, pp. 449–55; Fryde, pp. 117, 162.
23. W. Childs, 'England in Europe in the Reign of Edward II', in Dodd and Musson, pp. 97–118.
24. *Geoffrey le Baker*, p. 15.
25. Haines, p. 40; *The War of Saint-Sardos: Gascon Correspondence and Diplomatic Documents*, ed. P. Chaplais, Camden Third Series, vol. 87 (London: Royal Historical Society, 1954), pp. vii–xiii.
26. *Vita*, p. 235.

27. *Vita*, p. 243; *Anonimalle*, p. 119. It has been suggested, although without evidence, that Despenser might have attempted some act of 'sexual misconduct' with Isabella (P. Doherty, *Isabella and the Strange Death of Edward II* (London: Constable, 2003), p. 101).

28. *Vita*, p. 187.

29. *Geoffrey le Baker*, p. 20.

30. Quoted in Phillips, p. 489.

31. *Brut*, p. 237.

32. 'Annales Paulini', in Stubbs, I, p. 315; Buck, *Politics, Finance and the Church*, p. 218.

33. 'Annales Paulini', in Stubbs, I, p. 321.

34. 'Annales Bridlingtoniensis', in Stubbs, II, p. 87.

35. Phillips, p. 514.

36. *Brut*, p. 240.

37. British Library, London, MS Cotton Nero A.iv, folio 57v.

38. *Brut*, p. 240; *Geoffrey le Baker*, p. 24; *Lanercost*, p. 253.

39. *Select Documents*, pp. 37–8.

40. *Geoffrey le Baker*, pp. 26–7; Phillips, pp. 533–9.

41. J. Barlow, R. Bryant, C. Heighway, C. Jeens and D. Smith, *Edward II: His Last Months and His Monument* (Bristol: Bristol & Gloucestershire Archaeological Society and Past Historic, 2015), pp. 1–48.

42. *Geoffrey le Baker*, p. 32.

43. Phillips, p. 552.

5. IMAGINING EDWARD

1. *Parliament Rolls of Medieval England*, IV: *Edward III, 1327–1348*, ed. Seymour Phillips and Mark Ormrod, p. 104.

2. I. Mortimer, *Medieval Intrigue: Decoding Royal Conspiracies* (London: Continuum, 2010), pp. 61–151; Phillips, pp. 577–600; Haines, pp. 219–38.

3. *Parliament Rolls of Medieval England*, IV, pp. 11–12.

4. *Polychronicon Ranulphi Higden*, ed. Lumby, VIII, pp. 324–6.

5. Quoted in W. M. Ormrod, 'The Sexualities of Edward II', and I. Mortimer, 'Sermons of Sodomy: A Reconsideration of Edward II's Sodomitical Reputation', in Dodd and Musson, pp. 22–47, 48–60.

6. C. Given-Wilson, 'Richard II, Edward II, and the Lancastrian Inheritance', *English Historical Review* 109 (1994), pp. 553–71.

7. C. Marlowe, *Edward the Second*, ed. W. Moelwyn Merchant (London: Ernest Benn, 1967), pp. xiv–xxv and V.v.30.

8. Quoted in Phillips, 'The Reputation of a King', p. 51.

9. Marlowe, *Edward the Second*, ed. Merchant, V.v.113.

10. Marlowe, *Edward the Second*, ed. Merchant, p. xvi.

Further Reading

The most authoritative and balanced biography of Edward II is J. R. S. Phillips, *Edward II* (New Haven, Conn., and London: Yale University Press, 2010). R. M. Haines, *King Edward II: Edward of Caernarfon, His Life, His Reign, and Its Aftermath, 1284–1330* (Montreal and London: McGill-Queen's University Press, 2003), is less comprehensive but strong in certain areas, notably the king's relations with the episcopacy. The king's boyhood and upbringing are examined in detail in H. Johnstone, *Edward of Carnarvon, 1284–1307* (Manchester: Manchester University Press, 1946), and the standard biography of his father is M. Prestwich, *Edward I* (Berkeley, Calif.: University of California Press, 1988). *The Reign of Edward II: New Perspectives*, edited by G. Dodd and A. Musson (Woodbridge: York Medieval Press, 2006), is a thought-provoking collection of essays.

As well as the king, many of the chief figures of the reign have found their biographers. The almost simultaneous publication in the early 1970s of J. R. Maddicott, *Thomas of Lancaster 1307–1322: A Study in the Reign of Edward II* (Oxford: Oxford University Press, 1970), and J. R. S. Phillips, *Aymer de Valence, Earl of Pembroke, 1307–1324: Baronial Politics in the Reign of Edward II* (Oxford: Oxford University Press, 1972), swept away the 'constitutional' approach to the politics of the reign and brought the focus to bear on familial and territorial disputes. Gaveston's career and relationship with Edward are examined, with significant differences of emphasis, in J. Hamilton, *Piers Gaveston, Earl of Cornwall, 1307–1312: Politics and Patronage in the Reign of Edward II* (Detroit and London:

Wayne State University Press, 1988), and P. Chaplais, *Piers Gaveston: Edward II's Adoptive Brother* (Oxford: Clarendon Press, 1994). There are pacy biographies of Queen Isabella and Roger Mortimer: P. Doherty, *Isabella and the Strange Death of Edward II* (London: Constable, 2003), and I. Mortimer, *The Greatest Traitor: The Life of Sir Roger Mortimer, 1st Earl of March, Ruler of England 1327–1330* (London: Jonathan Cape, 2003), both of whom doubt that Edward was murdered in Berkeley Castle in 1327, although their conjectures as to his eventual fate are very different. The best accounts of the Younger Despenser's activities are N. Fryde, *The Tyranny and Fall of Edward II, 1321–1326* (Cambridge: Cambridge University Press, 1979), and M. Buck, *Politics, Finance and the Church in the Reign of Edward II: Walter Stapeldon, Treasurer of England* (Cambridge: Cambridge University Press, 1983), which provide detailed accounts of the last years of Edward's reign. The king's imprisonment at Berkeley Castle and his tomb in Gloucester Cathedral are thoroughly analysed in J. Barlow, R. Bryant, C. Heighway, C. Jeens and D. Smith, *Edward II: His Last Months and His Monument* (Bristol: Bristol & Gloucestershire Archaeological Society and Past Historic, 2015).

For Robert Bruce, it is still well worth reading G. W. S. Barrow, *Robert Bruce and the Community of the Realm of Scotland* (Edinburgh: Edinburgh University Press, 1965; third edition 1988), but see now also M. Penman, *Robert the Bruce, King of the Scots* (New Haven, Conn., and London: Yale University Press, 2014). Bannockburn is admirably contextualized by M. Brown, *Bannockburn: The Scottish War and the British Isles, 1307–1323* (Edinburgh: Edinburgh University Press, 2008). The fullest account of the Scottish impact on northern England and Ireland is C. McNamee, *The Wars of the Bruces: Scotland, England and Ireland 1306–1328* (East Linton: Tuckwell Press, 1997). For the geopolitics and ethnic complexity of Wales at this time, see R. R. Davies, *Lordship and Society in the March of Wales, 1278–1400* (Oxford: Oxford University Press, 1978). For the European famine of 1315–17, see W. C. Jordan, *The*

Great Famine: Northern Europe in the Early Fourteenth Century (Princeton, NJ: Princeton University Press, 1996), and for the impact of government policies on the peasantry, J. R. Maddicott, *The English Peasantry and the Demands of the Crown, 1294–1341, Past and Present* Supplement No. 1 (Oxford: Past and Present Society, 1975).

The two most interesting chronicles of the reign are (for court politics) *Vita Edwardi Secundi: The Life of Edward the Second*, edited and translated by W. R. Childs, Oxford Medieval Texts (Oxford: Clarendon Press, 2005), and (for northern affairs) *The Chronicle of Lanercost, 1272–1346*, edited and translated by Sir Herbert Maxwell (Glasgow: Glasgow University Press, 1913). Most of the key documents of the reign are collected in *English Historical Documents*, III: *1189–1327*, edited by H. Rothwell (London: Eyre and Spottiswoode, 1975). There is also a collection of Edward II's early letters: *Letters of Edward Prince of Wales, 1304–1305*, edited by H. Johnstone (Cambridge: Roxburghe Club, 1931).

Picture Credits

1. Effigy of Edward II, Gloucester Cathedral, c.1330s (Alamy)
2. Edward created Prince of Wales by his father, King Edward I, 1301. Illustration from Matthew Paris, *Chronica Roffense*, fourteenth century (British Library, London, Cotton Nero D. II, fol. 191v/British Library/Bridgeman Images)
3. Marriage of Edward II and Isabella of France in 1308. Detail of a miniature from Jean de Wavrin, *Chroniques d'Angleterre*, c.1475 (© Bibliothèque Nationale de France, Paris/MS Fr. 75, fol. 282)
4. Marcus Stone, *Edward II and Gaveston*, 1872 (Sotheby's/akg-images)
5. Guy de Beauchamp, Earl of Warwick, trampling the decapitated Piers Gaveston. Detail from an illustrated armorial roll-chronicle by John Rous, c.1483 (British Library, London, Add MS 48976/© The British Library Board, All Rights Reserved)
6. The Battle of Bannockburn, illustration from the *Scotichronicon* (vol. 2), c.1440 (Corpus Christi College, Cambridge, MS 171B, fol. 265r/The Master and Fellows of Corpus Christi College, Cambridge)
7. Head of Robert Bruce, reconstructed from his skull, by Brian Hill in 1996 (Scottish National Portrait Gallery)
8. The execution of Thomas, Earl of Lancaster in 1322. Miniature from the Luttrell Psalter, English School, 1325–5 (British Library, Add MS 42130, fol. 56/British Library, London/Bridgeman Images)

Index

Penguin Monarchs

THE HOUSES OF WESSEX AND DENMARK

Athelstan*	Tom Holland
Aethelred the Unready	Richard Abels
Cnut	Ryan Lavelle
Edward the Confessor	David Woodman

THE HOUSES OF NORMANDY, BLOIS AND ANJOU

William I*	Marc Morris
William II*	John Gillingham
Henry I	Edmund King
Stephen*	Carl Watkins
Henry II*	Richard Barber
Richard I*	Thomas Asbridge
John	Nicholas Vincent

THE HOUSE OF PLANTAGENET

Henry III*	Stephen Church
Edward I*	Andy King
Edward II*	Christopher Given-Wilson
Edward III*	Jonathan Sumption
Richard II*	Laura Ashe

THE HOUSES OF LANCASTER AND YORK

Henry IV	Catherine Nall
Henry V*	Anne Curry
Henry VI*	James Ross
Edward IV*	A. J. Pollard
Edward V	Thomas Penn
Richard III	Rosemary Horrox

* Now in paperback

THE HOUSE OF TUDOR

Henry VII	Sean Cunningham
Henry VIII*	John Guy
Edward VI*	Stephen Alford
Mary I*	John Edwards
Elizabeth I*	Helen Castor

THE HOUSE OF STUART

James I*	Thomas Cogswell
Charles I*	Mark Kishlansky
[Cromwell*	David Horspool]
Charles II*	Clare Jackson
James II*	David Womersley
William III & Mary II*	Jonathan Keates
Anne	Richard Hewlings

THE HOUSE OF HANOVER

George I*	Tim Blanning
George II	Norman Davies
George III	Amanda Foreman
George IV	Stella Tillyard
William IV*	Roger Knight
Victoria*	Jane Ridley

THE HOUSES OF SAXE-COBURG & GOTHA AND WINDSOR

Edward VII*	Richard Davenport-Hines
George V*	David Cannadine
Edward VIII*	Piers Brendon
George VI*	Philip Ziegler
Elizabeth II*	Douglas Hurd

* Now in paperback

ALLEN LANE
an imprint of
PENGUIN BOOKS

Also Published

Stephen Kotkin, *Stalin, Vol. II: Waiting for Hitler, 1928-1941*

Lindsey Fitzharris, *The Butchering Art: Joseph Lister's Quest to Transform the Grisly World of Victorian Medicine*

Serhii Plokhy, *Lost Kingdom: A History of Russian Nationalism from Ivan the Great to Vladimir Putin*

Mark Mazower, *What You Did Not Tell: A Russian Past and the Journey Home*

Lawrence Freedman, *The Future of War: A History*

Niall Ferguson, *The Square and the Tower: Networks, Hierarchies and the Struggle for Global Power*

Matthew Walker, *Why We Sleep: The New Science of Sleep and Dreams*

Edward O. Wilson, *The Origins of Creativity*

John Bradshaw, *The Animals Among Us: The New Science of Anthropology*

David Cannadine, *Victorious Century: The United Kingdom, 1800-1906*

Leonard Susskind and Art Friedman, *Special Relativity and Classical Field Theory*

Maria Alyokhina, *Riot Days*

Oona A. Hathaway and Scott J. Shapiro, *The Internationalists: And Their Plan to Outlaw War*

Chris Renwick, *Bread for All: The Origins of the Welfare State*

Anne Applebaum, *Red Famine: Stalin's War on Ukraine*

Richard McGregor, *Asia's Reckoning: The Struggle for Global Dominance*

Chris Kraus, *After Kathy Acker: A Biography*

Clair Wills, *Lovers and Strangers: An Immigrant History of Post-War Britain*

Odd Arne Westad, *The Cold War: A World History*

Max Tegmark, *Life 3.0: Being Human in the Age of Artificial Intelligence*

Jonathan Losos, *Improbable Destinies: How Predictable is Evolution?*

Chris D. Thomas, *Inheritors of the Earth: How Nature Is Thriving in an Age of Extinction*

Chris Patten, *First Confession: A Sort of Memoir*

James Delbourgo, *Collecting the World: The Life and Curiosity of Hans Sloane*

Naomi Klein, *No Is Not Enough: Defeating the New Shock Politics*

Ulrich Raulff, *Farewell to the Horse: The Final Century of Our Relationship*

Slavoj Žižek, *The Courage of Hopelessness: Chronicles of a Year of Acting Dangerously*

Patricia Lockwood, *Priestdaddy: A Memoir*

Ian Johnson, *The Souls of China: The Return of Religion After Mao*

Stephen Alford, *London's Triumph: Merchant Adventurers and the Tudor City*

Hugo Mercier and Dan Sperber, *The Enigma of Reason: A New Theory of Human Understanding*

Stuart Hall, *Familiar Stranger: A Life Between Two Islands*

Allen Ginsberg, *The Best Minds of My Generation: A Literary History of the Beats*

Sayeeda Warsi, *The Enemy Within: A Tale of Muslim Britain*

Alexander Betts and Paul Collier, *Refuge: Transforming a Broken Refugee System*

Robert Bickers, *Out of China: How the Chinese Ended the Era of Western Domination*

Erica Benner, *Be Like the Fox: Machiavelli's Lifelong Quest for Freedom*

William D. Cohan, *Why Wall Street Matters*

David Horspool, *Oliver Cromwell: The Protector*

Daniel C. Dennett, *From Bacteria to Bach and Back: The Evolution of Minds*

Derek Thompson, *Hit Makers: How Things Become Popular*

Harriet Harman, *A Woman's Work*

Wendell Berry, *The World-Ending Fire: The Essential Wendell Berry*

Daniel Levin, *Nothing but a Circus: Misadventures among the Powerful*

Stephen Church, *Henry III: A Simple and God-Fearing King*

Pankaj Mishra, *Age of Anger: A History of the Present*

Graeme Wood, *The Way of the Strangers: Encounters with the Islamic State*

Michael Lewis, *The Undoing Project: A Friendship that Changed the World*

John Romer, *A History of Ancient Egypt, Volume 2: From the Great Pyramid to the Fall of the Middle Kingdom*

Andy King, *Edward I: A New King Arthur?*

Thomas L. Friedman, *Thank You for Being Late: An Optimist's Guide to Thriving in the Age of Accelerations*

John Edwards, *Mary I: The Daughter of Time*

Grayson Perry, *The Descent of Man*

Deyan Sudjic, *The Language of Cities*

Norman Ohler, *Blitzed: Drugs in Nazi Germany*

Carlo Rovelli, *Reality Is Not What It Seems: The Journey to Quantum Gravity*

Catherine Merridale, *Lenin on the Train*

Susan Greenfield, *A Day in the Life of the Brain: The Neuroscience of Consciousness from Dawn Till Dusk*

Christopher Given-Wilson, *Edward II: The Terrors of Kingship*

Emma Jane Kirby, *The Optician of Lampedusa*

Minoo Dinshaw, *Outlandish Knight: The Byzantine Life of Steven Runciman*

Candice Millard, *Hero of the Empire: The Making of Winston Churchill*

Christopher de Hamel, *Meetings with Remarkable Manuscripts*

Brian Cox and Jeff Forshaw, *Universal: A Guide to the Cosmos*

Ryan Avent, *The Wealth of Humans: Work and Its Absence in the Twenty-first Century*

Jodie Archer and Matthew L. Jockers, *The Bestseller Code*

Cathy O'Neil, *Weapons of Math Destruction: How Big Data Increases Inequality and Threatens Democracy*

Peter Wadhams, *A Farewell to Ice: A Report from the Arctic*

Richard J. Evans, *The Pursuit of Power: Europe, 1815-1914*

Anthony Gottlieb, *The Dream of Enlightenment: The Rise of Modern Philosophy*

Marc Morris, *William I: England's Conqueror*

Gareth Stedman Jones, *Karl Marx: Greatness and Illusion*

J.C.H. King, *Blood and Land: The Story of Native North America*

Robert Gerwarth, *The Vanquished: Why the First World War Failed to End, 1917-1923*

Joseph Stiglitz, *The Euro: And Its Threat to Europe*

John Bradshaw and Sarah Ellis, *The Trainable Cat: How to Make Life Happier for You and Your Cat*

A J Pollard, *Edward IV: The Summer King*

Erri de Luca, *The Day Before Happiness*

Diarmaid MacCulloch, *All Things Made New: Writings on the Reformation*

Daniel Beer, *The House of the Dead: Siberian Exile Under the Tsars*

Tom Holland, *Athelstan: The Making of England*

Christopher Goscha, *The Penguin History of Modern Vietnam*

Mark Singer, *Trump and Me*

Roger Scruton, *The Ring of Truth: The Wisdom of Wagner's Ring of the Nibelung*

Ruchir Sharma, *The Rise and Fall of Nations: Ten Rules of Change in the Post-Crisis World*

Jonathan Sumption, *Edward III: A Heroic Failure*

Daniel Todman, *Britain's War: Into Battle, 1937-1941*

Dacher Keltner, *The Power Paradox: How We Gain and Lose Influence*

Tom Gash, *Criminal: The Truth About Why People Do Bad Things*

Brendan Simms, *Britain's Europe: A Thousand Years of Conflict and Cooperation*

Slavoj Žižek, *Against the Double Blackmail: Refugees, Terror, and Other Troubles with the Neighbours*

Lynsey Hanley, *Respectable: The Experience of Class*

Piers Brendon, *Edward VIII: The Uncrowned King*

Matthew Desmond, *Evicted: Poverty and Profit in the American City*

T.M. Devine, *Independence or Union: Scotland's Past and Scotland's Present*

Seamus Murphy, *The Republic*

Jerry Brotton, *This Orient Isle: Elizabethan England and the Islamic World*

Srinath Raghavan, *India's War: The Making of Modern South Asia, 1939-1945*

Clare Jackson, *Charles II: The Star King*

Nandan Nilekani and Viral Shah, *Rebooting India: Realizing a Billion Aspirations*

Sunil Khilnani, *Incarnations: India in 50 Lives*

Helen Pearson, *The Life Project: The Extraordinary Story of Our Ordinary Lives*

Ben Ratliff, *Every Song Ever: Twenty Ways to Listen to Music Now*

Richard Davenport-Hines, *Edward VII: The Cosmopolitan King*

Peter H. Wilson, *The Holy Roman Empire: A Thousand Years of Europe's History*

Todd Rose, *The End of Average: How to Succeed in a World that Values Sameness*

Frank Trentmann, *Empire of Things: How We Became a World of Consumers, from the Fifteenth Century to the Twenty-First*

Laura Ashe, *Richard II: A Brittle Glory*

John Donvan and Caren Zucker, *In a Different Key: The Story of Autism*

Jack Shenker, *The Egyptians: A Radical Story*

Tim Judah, *In Wartime: Stories from Ukraine*

Serhii Plokhy, *The Gates of Europe: A History of Ukraine*

Robin Lane Fox, *Augustine: Conversions and Confessions*

Peter Hennessy and James Jinks, *The Silent Deep: The Royal Navy Submarine Service Since 1945*

Sean McMeekin, *The Ottoman Endgame: War, Revolution and the Making of the Modern Middle East, 1908–1923*

Charles Moore, *Margaret Thatcher: The Authorized Biography, Volume Two: Everything She Wants*

Dominic Sandbrook, *The Great British Dream Factory: The Strange History of Our National Imagination*

Larissa MacFarquhar, *Strangers Drowning: Voyages to the Brink of Moral Extremity*

Niall Ferguson, *Kissinger: 1923-1968: The Idealist*

Carlo Rovelli, *Seven Brief Lessons on Physics*

Tim Blanning, *Frederick the Great: King of Prussia*

Ian Kershaw, *To Hell and Back: Europe, 1914–1949*

Pedro Domingos, *The Master Algorithm: How the Quest for the Ultimate Learning Machine Will Remake Our World*

David Wootton, *The Invention of Science: A New History of the Scientific Revolution*